D0481951

WITHDRAWN
UTSA LIBRARIES

Words Are Weapons

Inside ISIS's Rhetoric of Terror

Philippe-Joseph Salazar

Translation by Dorna Khazeni

Yale UNIVERSITY PRESS

New Haven & London

Library
University of Texas
at San Antonio

Published with assistance from the foundation established in memory of Amasa Stone Mather of the Class of 1907, Yale College.

English translation copyright © 2017 by Yale University.
Originally published as *Paroles armées: Comprendre et combattre la propagande terroriste*. © Lemieux Éditeur, 2015.
Published by arrangement with Patricia Pasqualini Literary Agency.

All rights reserved.

This book may not be reproduced, in whole or in part, including illustrations, in any form (beyond that copying permitted by Sections 107 and 108 of the U.S. Copyright Law and except by reviewers for the public press), without written permission from the publishers.

Yale University Press books may be purchased in quantity for educational, business, or promotional use. For information, please e-mail sales.press@yale.edu (U.S. office) or sales@yaleup.co.uk (U.K. office).

Set in Janson Roman type by Integrated Publishing Solutions.
Printed in the United States of America.

Library of Congress Control Number: 2016963572
ISBN 978-0-300-22322-4 (hardcover : alk. paper)

A catalogue record for this book is available from the British Library.

This paper meets the requirements of ANSI/NISO Z39.48-1992 (Permanence of Paper).

10 9 8 7 6 5 4 3 2 1

Library
University of Texas
at San Antonio

For Erik Doxtader, who pointed out that ISIS is the doubling in capital letters of the verb *to be* in the third person: ISIS, is, is, is, is . . .

Contents

Contents

Words Are Weapons

The Caliphate's Rhetorical Power

Cedant arma togae. This is the byword of many a pacifist illusion: that weapons yield to words. But it is an optical illusion. Weapons love words. With words they make new weapons.

Since the public massacres of the past few years (throat-slittings of journalists, humanitarian volunteers, and other imprudent individuals; the persecution of those minorities that defy an out-and-out version of Mohammedanism; the numerous actual or thwarted attacks in Europe and the United States) and the destruction of antiquities, the Western public, generally ignorant of the fact that acts of terror unfold daily in states under the control of the Caliphate,[1] has nonetheless come to realize that words accompany both the deeds by these militants on the ground and the massacres by its partisans in our territory.[2]

After inspiring and then celebrating bloody reprisals against

Charlie Hebdo in Paris on January 7, 2015, the Caliphate followed with a second salvo, this time of words—against the backdrop of the Eiffel Tower—calling on its partisans to undertake further attacks on the "accursed" French soil:

> There is a time for everything, a time to live, a time to die, a time to weep, a time to laugh, a time to love, a time to hate, the time has come to act and to save the religion with the tongue, the heart, the limbs, the pen, and the sword.[3]

The pen and the sword, indeed. The vituperations and attacks came as a surprise. Then, in Paris again, came November 13, 2015. Why were the French so startled at seeing violent Islam erupt among them? In reality France has been rubbing shoulders with Islam practically since its founding; France's first literary monument, and the first European epic poem, is the *Song of Roland*, a recitation of the valiant knight's sacrifice of his life to halt the advance of the Saracens on August 15, 778, the day of the Assumption of the Blessed Virgin. French literature is probably the richest in Europe on the topic of Muhammad:[4] The Koran was first translated into a European language by a Benedictine monk, Peter the Venerable, Abbot of Cluny, in Burgundy in the twelfth century. And yet, from one century to the next, in the face of the Muslim discourse, the French are stunned, oblivious each time to the multiple lessons of this long and difficult acquaintance. But they are not alone in being puzzled.

Indeed, the Western public is often disconcerted by the "oratory material" of Islam, and it is by this means that we can approach the first question this book raises, namely, how are we to understand the oratory and persuasive power of jihadism, and of the Caliphate in particular?

Allahu Akbar

First, we must grasp the rhetorical importance of the Muslim proclamation of faith (the *shahada*).[5] It is at once exemplary (to its faithful) and unusual (relative to other faiths). Islam is a religion to which one adheres by affirming (or by hearing recited, at birth) a laconic formula: "I attest that there is no god but *Allah*, and that Muhammad is his prophet." Entering Christianity, on the other hand, requires preparation, catechisms, conversations with a priest or pastor, baptism: in short, a series of at times lengthy, deliberate actions that are subject to scrutiny. Entering Islam is a powerful and dazzling act of language.[6] To be precise, the word *koran* means "recitation," and by the same token it is in the nature of the Muslim rhetorical model to be verbal, oratorical, declarative.

The laconic simplicity of the Muslim profession of faith (accompanied by an ablution) is an essential constituent of the Islamic State's call to action, and of jihadism.[7] It forms the basis for all action as it attests to the uniqueness of the Muslim god and the truthfulness of the prophetic words transcribed in the Koran. It is concentrated and contained in the "god is greater" chant that punctuates the actions of urban guerrillas as well as military engagements. It is amplified and grows in complexity in the harangues by the Caliphate's militants during beheadings or executions. The brevity of the declaration of faith that is repeated in the chant of faith and the eloquence of the harangues that make a case for the declaration of faith, therefore, go hand in hand.

To grasp the compelling but habitual power of *Allahu akbar,* one need only watch the videos of throat-slittings, stonings, defenestrations, and crucifixions, punctuated simply by these two words: judiciary episodes in the daily life of those cities under the administration of the Caliphate, with people looking on as they go about their grocery shopping or endure their banal traffic jams.

These executions are, in effect, licit acts, acts of justice: They are the proof and illustration that the profession of faith is functioning in the execution of the victim, just as a militant undertaking a suicide attack commits it as an act of faith. It is an indication of our confusion regarding the verbalization of these acts that, out of carelessness, the media employ the word *martyr:* A martyr, in Islam, perishes while committing an act of violence; a martyr, in Christianity, and this is the habitual meaning, does not commit violence but submits to violence.

One need only consult forums and blogs: Those who mock the soldiers and partisans' compulsive cries of *Allahu akbar* as a sign of guttural idiocy or of political illiteracy or as the cries of savages—because the formulation is short, it is repetitive, it is mechanical and does not tell us much—fail to understand that it is sufficient unto itself as it reasserts the very short initial declaration of faith that installs *jihad* at the center of the world. In the battle that we are told is being waged against Islamist or Islamic radicalization, as long as we fail to understand that the values of the Republic no longer have the same canonical and categorical force as the formulas of Mohammedan faith,[8] we will fall short in our arsenal of words.

To return to the French attitude facing Islamic terror, we cannot expect from them a return to the rhetorical sources of the French Republic in arms and assert with conviction and dare implement the watchword of the French Revolutionary Saint-Just: "No freedom for the enemies of freedom." Or that of the leader of the Terror himself, Robespierre: "If they invoke the heavens, it is to usurp the earth." And that of the extremist, Marat: "It is by violence that one must establish freedom." Henceforth, no one. Only, ironically, the Caliphate.

Still, the only way of combatting a rhetorical model is by understanding how it works—if we wish to confine ourselves to the arsenal of words alone.

The Power of the Oratorical Arabesque

Secondly, the brilliant force of the brief profession of faith allies itself to the power cultivated through political and militant grandiloquence that is also seen in the harangues accompanying the executions and in the Caliphate's proselytizing publications and videos.[9]

It is worth noting that Arabo-Islamic oratory is distinct among the various oratorical traditions (Indo-European, Sino-Japanese, Amerindian, Buddhist, etc.) for its florid style, so abundant in allegory, ornament, and formulas that seem exaggerated to us, and for its repetition and circumlocution, in imitation of the arabesques found in its mosaics. It is an illustrative display of oratory that, to us, sounds over the top.

Even if the Koran asserts that it was dictated in "an Arabic tongue that is easy to comprehend" (Sura 26, 195), it is still true that Arab-Islamic rhetoric bears the stamp of moral allegory, evident in the titles of the suras in the Koran ("The Bee," "The Spider") in the foundational text and that the Koranic style acts as an intravenous drip nourishing an entire linguistic ecology.

Witness to the primacy of oratory in Islamic culture, Khomeini,[10] in his eloquent *Final Discourse* (1983)[11] designates the collection of military harangues and exhortative speeches by Ali, the founder of Shi'ism, as "the greatest book after the Koran," thus placing on the same plane a work of human oratory and the sacred word,[12] persuasive human words and divine words.[13] The implication that follows is that human persuasion serves to concretize divine injunctions. Human persuasion serves to make actionable what would otherwise remain literary, mystical.

Arabo-Islamic oratorical art rendered in contemporary West-

ern vernacular sounds grandiloquent and slightly outdated to
our ears:

> The blood of martyrs, the tears of the pious and the ink of the
> sages did not flow in vain, the Caliphate has been restored by
> a small gathering of the faithful and its banner has now been
> hoisted high in spite of trials, tempests and treacheries.[14]

This is a poetic style that, out of its cultural context, rings false.
But it is veridical, it allows the expression of a truth.

In fact, an important treatise on the rhetoric of Islamic civilization devotes three quarters of its analysis to stylistic devices,
enigmas, and allusions. Their use as levers of refinement in argumentation is both dazzling and systematic.[15]

Islamic oratorical art is ornamentation, but of a methodical
type whose aim is cognitive, just as the arabesque is both decora-
tive (its skillful salient curve) and didactic (its incorporation of a
Koranic citation): The arabesque exists to support a battery of
logic; under its efflorescence the pictorial style conceals a dialectical weapon. Ornament is instructive.

Didactic indeed, for early in its history, philosophy in the Islamic territories integrated rhetoric and poetics with the logic
of Aristotle, some of whose texts it had assimilated by twisting
them in an attempt at reconciliation with the Koran.[16]

Hence the integration of rhetoric, with its arguments founded
on opinions governing coexistence (that is, politics), into a
logic system of rational or scientific arguments. And hence, to

a greater degree, the integration of poetics and the persuasive effects of an imagistic style (culture) into that system of rational arguments.[17]

In other words, a strong image, hammered repetition, and lyrical soaring combine to stand in for logical proof—in what is a radical departure from the Greek rationality whose successors we who reside in the Western intellectual and cultural tradition still are today. These elements not only help the process of interpreting sacred references,[18] they also assist in regulating daily life. Christian Europe, on the other hand, resisted a wish to rhyme the poetic and the rhetorical with logical reasoning: Herein lies one of the sources of European rationalism and its advances in the sciences.

The theological reason in Islam for this logico-rhetorico-poetic continuum is a consequence of the massive presence of "poetry" in the Koran, which, lest we forget, is a book dictated by a divine angel but also a book of law. It was necessary, therefore, to justify the fact that God spoke rhetorically and poetically. To exclude poetics and rhetoric from the social life and language of Muslims would amount to a rejection of the style of the Koran and would constitute a heresy. Therefore, rhetoric and poetics had to be injected into mental logical schemas.

So, what seems florid, exaggerated, poetic, and ostentatious to us in the harangues of the executioners does not appear so to those who speak in this manner and certainly does not to those who propagate the call to *jihad* and submission to the Caliphate.

Against this style we are disarmed: Our political language, in comparison, is sterile, rhetorically banal, and poetically deficient.

Therefore, in the Caliphate's discourse, there is a logic at work that is disjunctive relative to what we think of as logical, reasonable, and persuasive in politics. A logic of another order, a logic that appears perverse or delusional to us. But it is a logic that contains, aside from the profession of faith and its evocative poetic force, dialectical rigor: the rigor of analogical reasoning.

Analogy as Weapon of Logic

Resorting to analogy is contrary to Western habits of political discourse: An analogy is valuable as illustration but not as argument. Islam's rhetorical ecology maintains a radically opposite conception of this.

THE POWER OF ANALOGICAL NARRATIVES

In fact, in Islamic legal tradition, analogy is the fourth foundation of legal reasoning.

Drawn from the Koran and the *hadiths* (accounts of events involving Muhammad and of deeds by him, also known as "tradition"),[19] which are very often imagistic since they are material facts and concrete deeds, examples serve as the basis for resolving practical questions: The relationship established between an example drawn from tradition and a given question functions by analysis of an analogy, which, in turn, is a solution that is inscribed as a legal opinion, or *fatwa.*

For example, one might imagine this scene: The owner of a store realizes that his partners are fleecing him and that he is on the verge of bankruptcy. He must decide whom to get rid of, that is to say, he must determine the degree of each person's responsibility. When debating the subject of corruption, as is the case here, one can have recourse to a *hadith*, an account attributed to Muhammad, of a mouse who has fallen into some butter. The question is: Is the butter entirely soiled? Muhammad answered: "Throw out the mouse with all that surrounds it and eat your butter."[20] By analogy with this short tale, a doctor of faith whom the tradesman consults for guidance regarding to what degree it is reasonable to incriminate those responsible may counsel him (and this will be his legal opinion, a *fatwa*) that, just as the degree of corruption of a liquid depends on its consistency (that is to say, on the proximity of the cause of the corruption), one may settle for punishing only those who truly were the immediate cause of the bankruptcy.

This is just an example, but the tale and analogy are canonical—in the matter of determining what is illicit when considering a fungible good (like butter) where quantities are hard to determine.[21] This is how, by relying on the imagistic character of a story, analogical logic functions and exerts its political and public power.[22]

By using analogies in its propaganda, jihadist politics therefore feeds on a rhetorical ambiance that seems bizarre or irrational to us (one need only read a few blogs to observe the average Westerner's reaction to the phenomenon) but constitutes a powerful and generalized political form for interpreting things:

> what we do in interpreting is to move the meaning of a word from its proper sense to a figurative sense, without distorting the way the Arabic language uses figurative language: anything can be designated by its analogue, its cause, its effect. . . .[23]

This form of interpretation has a name: *ijtihad*.[24] It is all of a piece: Joining the Caliphate is an act of interpreting the world.

THE ANALOGY DETERMINES THE LEGAL

Analogical reasoning, therefore, allows a decision to be made about the licit and the illicit in politics,[25] for example whether beheading is legal or not or, to speak more precisely, licit or illicit.

The licit and the illicit are therefore not determined by the application of a norm of law and in an adversarial debate about facts (as in our legal tradition, which originates in Rome) but by the confrontation of tradition with analogical values in order to arrive at an interpretation:

> He that is named miscreant, his wealth is licit for Muslims and his blood may be spilled, his blood is the blood of the dog, no sin in spilling it, and no blood money need be paid.[26]

The political results can be stupefying, like the embrace offered by a perpetrator to his victim before the latter, accused of sodomy, is thrown off a tall building and stoned by the community as she is dying:[27] a "perverse" act according to Western media, a licit gesture, since punishment does not annul crime but restores the violator to the law and to the community:

> Were your sins to reach the clouds in the Heavens, and were you then to solicit my Pardon, I would accord it to you.[28]

The Caliphate and the Literal Reading of the Koran

The media, certain Western politicians, or Muslims living outside countries ruled by Islamic law hold forth on the "literal reading" of the Koran and of tradition by jihadists. They argue that a correct and an incorrect reading of the text exist, but they fail to refer to the essential element:[29] the analogy. The reading must be literal (citations from the Koran and tradition) in order for the analogy to take place, since analogical reasoning is always based on a literal fact (as with the mouse in the bowl of butter).

Those who refute the "literal reading" by jihadists and who uphold a concept of Koranic humanism[30] need to provide us with their own analogical interpretation of the suras or the *hadiths;* they need to tell us how, in view of these texts, the soldiers of the Caliphate are able to justify their interpretation in order to behead, to burn, to stone, to crucify, and simply to wage war against the world and how their own reading is different, for example, from the reading that legitimizes flagellations, mutilations, stonings, and beheadings in Saudi Arabia, an ally country.

Here we stand before a culture of analogical reasoning that we do not understand and that we, therefore, reduce to the alternative familiar to us: a literal (hence false) interpretation versus an interpretation open to debate (hence true). We fail to grasp the force of the analogy and how it animates the Caliphate's propaganda.

Analogy draws its force from a relationship that is at once imagistic (seducing the imagination), concrete (attaching itself to a given problem), and logical (without being abstract), that it establishes between two facts: one immersed in known and revered tradition and the other fixed in a concrete situation. This explains why a crowd gawks at a crucifixion. The crowd is neither passive nor cruel: It perceives the punishment as the result of an analogical judgment. In the same way we perceive a court order to proceed from a sum of evidence.

These then are the primary terms for words as weapons that structure the conquering rhetoric of the Caliphate.

The Western passion for deft ripostes and the art of adversarial debate, for the value accorded to dialogue among partners, and, in general, for the primacy accorded to self-expression, however, falters in the face of this other dominion of words as weapons.

Whether or not an effective military offensive annihilates the Caliphate's territory, we must rethink the rhetorical terms of this engagement and acknowledge that the confrontation starts with a rhetorical war in which the adversary controls a homogeneous panoply, moving from injunction to analogy, employing a compelling oratorical art, sustained by the powerful logistics of an interpretative legalism. Where negotiators are concerned, we need to grasp that sending diplomats who speak Arabic is not enough. We need Islamic speakers who can present arguments in Islamic, who can match the adversary's level of rhetoric.

ONE

The Caliph Speaks

The cultural distance separating us from the Caliphate's jihadism in space and time could be seen in the broad light of day in the summer of 2014 as the West was succumbing to the pleasures of its devotion to grand sports spectacles: cricket at Lord's, tennis at Wimbledon, soccer in Brazil, and the Tour de France. At that same moment, the Caliphate was being founded.

Al-Baghdadi[1] stood and intoned the homily for the reestablishment of the Caliphate in the very holy mosque of Mosul, the equivalent, in terms of pomp and circumstance, of a presidential inauguration,[2] and he became Caliph Ibrahim. Far from the stadiums, a Muslim consecration had come to pass, pivoting the jihadism of old on its hinges and flinging open the new gates of war.

In May 2015, while *Mad Max* (a fiction surpassed by reality) was all the rage at the Cannes Film Festival, Caliph Ibrahim, delivering his second address *urbi et orbi*, opened up the path of *hegira*, the emigration of good Muslims toward "the protective shadow of the Caliphate."[3]

At the time of his first appearance, from *Le Monde* to *The Wall Street Journal*, al-Baghdadi was mocked when he proclaimed the restoration of the Caliphate: "a masquerade," a "*mise en scène*."[4] To proselytization and to consecration we responded with the most juvenile rhetoric: sarcasm. The media have since been stripped of their illusions.

So what happened in Mosul on Friday, July 4, 2014, on Independence Day, by intentional coincidence?[5]

A Symbolic Strategy of Action

A rhetorical situation never shows its hand outright. For its workings to be seen, it must be dismantled.

THE CALIPH APPEARS

The faithful of every age and every condition stand in rows, facing the wall of the *mihrab* pointing to Mecca. He that bears the mantle of the Caliphate, wearing black like a Benedictine monk or a Greek pope, slowly mounts the steps that lead to the preacher's pulpit. He sits facing the faithful. A clock marks the time. Twenty minutes after noon. By twenty minutes to one the stupefying announcement has been concluded. The Caliphate has been restored.

No theatrics, no *mise en scène*, no sleight of hand. On the contrary, a dignity of carriage and a natural composure that immediately evoke the Prophet, in word and in gesture. The rhetorical effect of this apparition is magisterial.

These are early days for a symbolic strategy of action: A man become caliph.

Indeed, if the life of the caliph is known, this biography preceding his ascension to Mohammedan succession is simply that, a "biography," a curriculum vitae, a fact sheet.[6] With the proclamation, this biography becomes hagiography, a tradition of spoken words and of gestures that hereafter pertain to a holy history. His life story goes from a fact sheet to a holy legend.[7]

Of course, to our ear, such a religious argument is scandalous, but is it that different from what French schoolbooks say about the life of the secular yet hallowed figures of Napoleon Bonaparte and Socialist leader Jean Jaurès or, in the U.S. context, Washington or Lincoln? There is always a before and an after, divided by a caesura defined by a remarkable event that tips private biography to political hagiography. This implies that it is pointless to excavate the details of the man's biography: What matters is that he will henceforth speak as the caliph.

THE CALIPH SPEAKS

After a short invocation, Ibrahim stands and calmly delivers his sermon.[8] He assumes *ipso facto* the function of imam, in other words leads the prayer. Moreover, he explicitly evokes the *imam-*

ate, for this is the fundamental function of a Muslim sovereign: An imam is he who "stands facing" (the meaning of the term) the faithful in order to show them the way and to speak of the spiritual task at hand and the path to follow, *jihad*.

His eloquence is solemn, and the speech is delivered uninterrupted, without notes or a teleprompter. The sole oratorical gesture the caliph allows himself is a raised hand to mark points of emphasis, but there are not too many of them. The sermon, therefore, proceeds according to classical stylistic norms, alternating injunctions to fight for the faith with Koranic citations, and it is assisted by an eloquent and ceremonial diction cultivated by Koranic diction.[9] A great specimen of the art of oratory that shall become the rhetorical model for numerous harangues and declarations by the Caliphate.

The dignity of the oratorical performance is, indeed, that of a coronation, for as he speaks and leads the prayers with a reflection on "polytheism," on the need for eradicating faithlessness and against the temptation to succumb to it, he becomes the Commander of the Faithful. In rhetoric, such an operation is called "performative." By speaking what the Koran says, he who states it well, by demonstrating that others are "polytheists," assumes the Caliphate. He has "performed" the Caliphate. The Caliphate has come into existence. For all intents and purposes the Caliph's speech is doubly foundational, as a Muslim Independence Day speech and as a State of the Nation of Islam address, and this rhetorical compact should be coldly treated as such.

ADDRESSING THE POLYTHEISTS, US

"Polytheism" is a key element: The term defines the other public, not the one made up by the faithful, the one in the mosque, but the one that is the enemy.

Polytheism subsumes all of Western or Westernized culture: the worship of the "idols of the tribe" (media, cinema, celebrities, sports role models),[10] "the idols of the marketplace" (consumer goods, religious deviations from Islam that indulge in "pagan" mercantilism), "the idols of the theater" (the simulacra of knowledge, of communication, of technology), "the idols of the cavern" (each judging the world only through one's own narrow vision, blinkered by one's prejudices, outside the light of God), and in sum, democratic regimes that place human rights at the center of their system and hence make an idol of the Human.

The term *polytheistic*, repeated several times, is at the heart of the sermon, and to think it old-fashioned, theatrical, or verbose would be to misjudge its power. It is in the face of polytheistic multiplicity and duplicity that the wisdom of the true language of monotheism rises to be heard. And it is on this confrontation that caliphal assumption is founded.

NAMING POWER

Evidently, from Washington to Paris, we have a certain idea of what it means to seize power and what constitutes a state. We are having trouble naming the Caliphate (see chapter 3).

How is a state born? We frame the takeover of power according to codes that are considered evident: a revolution or coup d'état, legitimization through a general election, recognition by the U.N., a constitution, and, in certain cases, South America for example, we are even willing to make an allowance for "institutional coups d'état." In short, codified formulas for designating a state exist, even if international law is hesitant to provide a fixed definition and even if U.N. member states do not always agree on recognizing a new state.[11]

There also exists an obligatory political chain of events that involves the ritual of a presidential election. In the old days, a Constituent Assembly would first be formed; these days, it is a presidential election, as though this were some kind of remedy—more often it is pure poison. This chain of events, which also includes the presence of international observers and their acolytes—humanitarian missions—allows the head of a legitimate state to be designated. The establishment of a state follows certain political norms ("The habitual definition of a state is that of a community that consists of a territory and a population subject to political authority")[12] and rhetorical codes.

Whereas, at the venerable mosque of Mosul, nothing of the kind. There is a refusal to turn to procedures and terms normalized by the West and, for that matter, the world. Hence, the term for naming the political function of governing is *wali*. But if the *wilayah* is the authority emanating from military prowess at the service of faith, this service is historically led by the caliph, that is, by the man who takes charge of jihad. For whether or not a *wali*, or "governor," can or cannot be a caliph (such was the case in the past, both the distant past and more recently), the two functions can meld in the same individual who takes charge of the leadership of believers. So, is Ibrahim an imam (he is conducting the prayers), a *wali*, or an emir?[13] All three: a caliph. But through a procedure that does not correspond to our frameworks for seizing power.

Our political glossary, conveyed as it is by the media, is incapable of framing these notions and this procedure, of acclimatizing to them.

The assumption that occurred on Friday, July 4, therefore did so outside the framework of our modern political rhetoric. The contemptuous refusal of the new caliph to adorn himself with a title as head of state in the European manner signals a radical rupture with the leaders of the Middle East and the Maghreb who, since the end of the nineteenth century, have adopted Western forms of address (emperor, king, president). In his May 2015 speech, Caliph Ibrahim refers to the heads of state in the Arabo-Muslim world by the simple title of "governor," in the sense of those who govern—for the time being. Other than this derisive term, not a single title imitates the West. Even in forms of address, we do not speak the same political language.

Seizing Power through Language

So, then, we should say "caliph," but what does the word designate in terms of the power that has been seized?[14]

THE DEMAND FOR OBEDIENCE

Power may be assumed. Its seizure must nonetheless be secured.

The takeover of power here is of a rare kind, founded on a demand for "obedience" (see chapter 6). The caliph calls for obedience. This demand appears extravagant to us: The concept the term names, obedience, has simply vanished from our social glossary and from our political code. Our democratic systems have eradicated the idea of obedience, above all the obedience due to the Law, to the point of celebrating civil disobedience as duty. Everything is negotiable, everything is a dialogue (see chapter 5). To obey is obscene.

But then, here is a return of the repressed term. Caliph Ibrahim is neither crazy nor overly excited. He knows what he is saying to the faithful before him at the ancient mosque of Mosul: To obey is a political virtue, and this is how the seizure of power is decided. How can one ask for obedience to be granted? The request is rhetorically paradoxical, because to ask to be obeyed is to concede that this obedience can be refused, hence disobeyed, before it is even given.

The obedience that is naturally due the caliph: Here we are in deep, inside a radically exotic political universe. Railing against it is useless. We need to understand it. *The Wall Street Journal*, unwittingly, conveys the measure of our stupefaction by mocking the "self-appointed" caliph. Whereas, in fact, a caliph self-appoints. It is a duty, and this is how he establishes his legitimate demand for obedience. Explanation: In the political tradition of Islam, the world is divided in two, non-believers here and believers there; between the two groups, if the believer obeys God, there can only exist a state of war. This war is a result of the non-believer's refusal to abandon polytheism and its idols. It is a result of his radical disobedience. Our disobedience.

In other words, it is the proclamation of an absolute duty to obedience that drives both the *imamate*, the leading of prayers, and the Caliphate, the political leadership. The Caliph is, therefore, he who proclaims and takes on the expansion of the domain of faith for humanity, by asserting the duty of obedience.

The traditions extend this duty of obedience to *jihad* even to include "evil" Muslim potentates, bad princes. Those Islamic regimes that have imitated Western systems, profoundly or superficially, or that collaborate with miscreants are automatically disqualified, but it is incumbent upon them, nonetheless, to obey the superior imperative of *jihad*, or upon their people to overthrow them.

The rhetorical armature is unremitting among the duty to obey the word of God, the division between believers and non-believers, and what is necessarily a self-proclamation—and this is the moral basis for acts of insurrection in Yemen, in Libya, in Nigeria, and in the Caucasus.

In this vision, there is no dynastic or popular legitimacy inscribed in a fixed state-like entity—these are all Western concepts. There is only the immediate authority emanating from the one who shows believers the path to follow, a path that is forever expanding into the territorial domain of obedience. A Caliph acts as a successor to Muhammad in the pursuit of the expansion of the community or nation of believers, the one through whom *jihad* passes and transits, in a continuation of prophetic action.[15]

AN ISLAMIC "DECLARATION OF INDEPENDENCE"

This montage may appear extravagant, but is it any more so than the belief in the existence of a "general will" that lies at the heart of democratic regimes? Or the regular appeal to the "values of the republic," which, were they known or fixed, would probably make elections unnecessary by stimulating spontaneous obedience as a consequence of their effective virtue?

Getting back to the intentional coincidence of the dates of the caliphal proclamation and the American national holiday, let us reread the Declaration of Independence: A class of merchants and landowners, in power in the "rebel colonies" at the time, proclaimed that equality among men, liberty, the right to live, and access to happiness were "self-evident truths." Clearly, they were no more so then than the Caliphate's declaration is today, since it took a bloody revolution, the refusal on the part of the Loyalist population to submit to the Boston "agitators," two English invasions, an atrocious civil war, the continual subjugation of blacks up until the race riots and the civil rights movement, for this "self-evidence" to turn into political evidence. And yet, self-evidence was proclaimed, and a republic was born.

Do not underestimate the power of a proclamation: Two great model republics, the French and the American, were in fact constituted or anticipated by proclamations (the American Declaration, the Tennis Court Oath). At the time, political Europe laughed out loud,[16] and these entities, founded on the basis of a new language, were held in derision. But two republican states were the outcome, on two continents, that changed the course of history. Words "perform." Once the Caliphate has been declared, it exists. It is performative. The Caliphate's impact on the young men and women who convert and join this caliphal republic, for that is what it is, is contingent on its proclamatory nature that exerts the same idealistic force as did the Declaration of Independence or the Tennis Court Oath. It also elicits the same refutation from the political establishment.

We might as well accept the power of this proclamation. We might as well accept that words, in politics, have the power to create.[17]

We are dealing here with powerful rhetorical constructs that warn us never to imagine that everyone reasons as we do, frames politics as we frame it, or operates on the basis of the same commonplaces to which we are accustomed: We must evaluate the appearance of a new oratorical form in politics, as signaled by the emergence of a new rhetoric; it should command sustained attention and not ignorant disdain.

There will come a day where we will have to do what the Renaissance French King Francis I did, to the outrage of Christianity, when Turks were setting Hungary ablaze and awash in blood: He talked to the enemy. The king went so far as to allow the caliph's flotilla to winter near Toulon. The death of the caliph, assassinated by a drone, will change nothing at all: There will be a successor to his rhetoric.

We must, on the other hand, be realistic and prepare for a bellicose coexistence with the Caliphate's rhetorical power and thus relearn the iron rule of international relations that are not "relations," in the comforting sense of the word, but "rapports"— of force, to be precise. The Caliphate has put us back in realpolitik.[18] It is up to us to revise our glossaries. But the rhetorical terms for a political engagement are not invented on the fly. We must begin to reflect on the rhetorical means for a long-term political engagement with the Caliphate's rhetorical challenge, which goes far beyond the territorial existence of the Islamic State.

TWO

Naming the Territory of Terror

With the Caliphate, the world has entered a disequilibrium of terror. This disequilibrium is in part due to the rhetorical construction of terror and of territory. This is the topic of this chapter.

Noble, Protective Terror

The law is meant to furnish us with a stable glossary. It so happens, in the case of terror, that French law commits a strange blunder—its definition of terror is circular:

> The following offenses constitute acts of terrorism where they are committed intentionally in connection with an individual or collective undertaking the purpose of which is seriously to disturb public order through intimidation or terror. . . .[1]

The U.S. Code is just as circular, whether applied to international or domestic terrorism:

(1) the term "international terrorism" means activities that—

  (A) involve violent acts or acts dangerous to human life that are a violation of the criminal laws of the United States or of any State, or that would be a criminal violation if committed within the jurisdiction of the United States or of any State;

  (B) appear to be intended— (i) to intimidate or coerce a civilian population; (ii) to influence the policy of a government by intimidation or coercion; or (iii) to affect the conduct of a government by mass destruction, assassination, or kidnapping;

. . .

(5) the term "domestic terrorism" means activities that—

  (A) involve acts dangerous to human life that are a violation of the criminal laws of the United States or of any State; (B) appear to be intended— (i) to intimidate or coerce a civilian population; (ii) to influence the policy of a government by intimidation or coercion; or (iii) to affect the conduct of a government by mass destruction, assassination, or kidnapping.[2]

In other words, we do not possess a definition of *terror* in itself but a list of "offenses" or "activities" called "acts of terrorism." The legislator does not define *terror*. By replacing one word with another, it states that terror is constituted by an act of terrorism or violence. Where is the key definition?

So we are forced to turn to the venerable source of the law

and to its founding glossary, the Roman Digest. This source concerning terror is often cited secondhand in works of geopolitics, war studies, or political science but without providing a precise reference, to wit the jurist Pomponius.[3]

Pomponius's formula for defining *terror* is striking: Terror is what allows a magistrate to hold back a criminal by inspiring a "salutary fear" in him, and thus "the right to terrorize, that is, to expel out of the territory," is foundational to the integrity of an organized and sovereign people on its own territory —which remains the present definition of a state, as noted earlier.

"Terror" is, therefore, a noble and protective notion.

This right to terror consists, nonetheless, of two elements: a moral constituent, to inspire salutary fear, and a practical constituent, to maintain territorial integrity. We are beginning to discern a definition of terror that, contrary to the circular definition by legislators, does not force us around in circles but allows us to move forward.

Originally, therefore, it is the law that is terrorist, and it is this right to terrorize that maintains territory, by removing from it those deemed criminal, who threaten the borders of the common territory—physical borders, soon interpreted as abstract and ethical limits or violations that run the risk of turning into generalized strife on the territory and those residing therein.

The expression "balance of terror," in the age of nuclear dissuasion, was in keeping with Roman jurisprudence: The two blocs mutually terrorized each other for the safeguard of their territory, their sovereignty, their people, their state.

In sum, the meaning of the terrorist rhetorical montage is inspired by the legal notion of the benevolent custodian of social coexistence, but subjected to a violent twist by the Islamic State.

The Idealized Territory of Terrorism

The Caliphate's[4] terrorism differs from Al-Qaeda's: It is an international call for territory.[5] Question: What about the nature of terror's territory of action?[6]

In the case of old-fashioned terrorism—think anarchist insurrections and communist class struggle—the domain of action was the subject of discussions on strategy, on justified means, the validity of bombs, assassinations, machine gun attacks, and insurrections. Defining the domain of action and the just means of accomplishing it has always divided revolutionaries. Lenin was suspicious of adventurism, fearing it as too individualistic and too romantic.[7] Insurrections, coups d'états, yes. Terrorism, no, other than terror aimed at expelling and containing those who did not comply with the revolution (this was the original reason for the Gulag, the anti-territory). However, a given territory served as a bridgehead toward internationalization.

To sum up, a theoretico-practical distinction existed between terrorism (individual, anarchistic, romantic, and in the long term, ineffectual) and terror (collective, strategic, rational, and the engine of history), as a consequence of which the territory of the deployment of terror was subject to the strategy of the revolution, at a specific point in its bid for internationalization.

This game plays out differently in the era of jihadism.

Beginning with and following the attacks by Al-Qaeda on September 11, 2001, terrorism clearly served as a hyphen, a violent one, between two parts of the world, between the part of the world that is the community of believers and this other part, that is, the community of apostates, infidels, and idolaters.

But although *jihad,* according to the intellectual warrior Bin Laden, was an effort to convert the latter and turn them into the former by carrying the war there, it had no territorial aspirations. It operated from a multiplicity of locations and from a mobile base ("base" is the translation of *Al-Qaeda*). The "base" was in reality an operational headquarters but also a moral and religious base, a sort of battle monastery and a laboratory for "messages" from the scholar-soldier, the sheikh Bin Laden. We were in fact dealing with a refusal on the part of terrorism to territorialize. Everywhere and nowhere. The base in question had decided to strike New York and Washington, for this meant a strike against their base, the immoral base of the enemy: finance and power.[8]

In the chaos of the wars that followed September 11 and the hullaballoo around the manhunt, this dimension was forgotten.

One could say, one must say, that Bin Laden's vision was metaphysical: His speeches were similar, in their theological culture, in their sober handling of style, in the breadth of their vision and the beauty of their phraseology, to papal encyclicals or to Calvin's grand Protestant sermons: emphatic and prophetic messages calling the world to conversion.[9]

These messages from the base did not lay claim to a particular territory but to a true theological abstraction: the universe. The terrorist actions affirmed the value of the messages without aspiring to occupy material terrain. The action of the terror aimed to incite a sort of mental turmoil in apostates (Saudi Arabia, occupying holy sites since its conquest of Mecca and Medina in the 1920s, and the forced exile of their millennial protector, the Hashemite emir), in idolaters (Muslims that had sold out to Christians), and in infidels.

For Bin Laden a kind of metaphysics of terror existed: Terrorist action existed to force the blinders to fall away from eyes, to open minds to the truth, to reveal the justice of the Koran. In short, to proclaim the universal law. This terror, in the tradition of Roman law, existed to "inspire a salutary fear," that is, a fear that brings salvation to the soul.

Bin Laden's speeches were argument-based constructs that, again and again, hammered the same lesson home. One could even say the terrorist act was extraordinary: It supplanted the nonexistence of an army with "the cavalry of Islam" and their effectual presence on territory purified of apostasies and idolatries, itself a living example of the perfect universe, sublime and converted to Islam.

As paradoxical as it seems, Bin Laden's terrorism was a practice of salvation, functioning on an abstract territory of ethical dimensions, a metaphysical territory. We therefore find in it the moral constituent, issued from Roman law and evoked earlier, namely that to terrorize is just.

The Polymorphous Territory of the Caliphate

Arabo-Muslim civilization has known quite a few other territorial and ethnic permutations aimed at the control of territory,[10] but with the Caliphate's terrorism, we move to the second aspect of the ancient concept in Roman law, the practical aspect, for there exists an actual territory.

This territory is precisely the Caliphate, in all the term's ambiguity, since it designates, aside from the sacred dimension, a form of political management as well as a state (see chapter 13).

Let us note that for us, consumers of Western media, it is first a territory of words: Its proclamation was required for it to materialize and for the zone controlled by a group, at first called Al-Qaeda in Iraq (2004), then Islamic State of Iraq (2006), finally the Islamic State in Syria and the Levant (2013), to be constituted. Jihadists who undertake their *hegira* toward the Caliphate often simply refer to it as *al-dawlat*, "the state," with no qualifiers. Short. Absolute. The state. In the same manner the British say "the United Kingdom" or Americans "the United States" without any other qualification. Or the French "la République."

The Caliphate's Multidimensional Territory

On the one hand, the terror propagated is territorial: expelling all who persist in not converting, destroying everything that symbolizes apostasy or miscreancy (Western stores, churches, ancient statues), welcoming those that join the territory in order to fight or to leave behind the lands of immorality or to govern or to administer.

On the other hand, it serves as a territory for departures toward conquest; that is to say, it exists also to terrorize non-Muslims outside their own territory.[11] The Caliphate expresses a right of ownership and a right of conquest where terrorist acts are not extraterritorial but an assertion of ownership over all territory, a re-conquest.

And thirdly, a land "of redemption" toward which good Muslims who are "well guided" (a true Caliph is himself a guide who is indeed "well guided") must emigrate in order to live decent lives:[12] paradoxically (in our eyes), those who undertake the *hegira* toward the Caliphate flee the terror of enslavement to the customs of Westerners (see chapter 7), even while terrorizing them outside their own territory.[13] The return to the sacred land of Islam is a repentance and a return to God, a favorite theme of the Caliphate's publications:[14]

> All sincere Muslims emigrate toward one of the regions of the Islamic State, this land of *Islam*, and shall leave the lands of the miscreants, led by the worst *tawaghit* [idolaters] in this world, that make endless war on our community. It is now the turn

of the believers to advance, to recover lands, and to not leave these tyrants a single second of rest. No Muslim can remain far from this land without being assailed by regret and without wishing to come to it so as to be closer to their God.[15]

SYMBOLIC APPROPRIATION

The territorial argument of terror, therefore, goes something like this: Because France already belongs to the Caliphate but is occupied by miscreants, we must terrorize them, inspire a salutary fear in them, and if they do not respect the integrity of Islam and refuse to convert, we must chase them away, keep them out.

To murder in London, Paris, Copenhagen, Sydney, Orlando is a way of underscoring that the territory we live in already belongs to the Caliphate. This is why the Caliphate's communications strategists name combatants that join the caliphal territories by appending their places of origin to their new Islamic name, or urge them to do so, hence Abou Shahrazaad al-Narwegi, from Norway;[16] Nicholas Rovinski, known as Nuh Amrik,[17] from America; Romain Letellier becomes Abou Siyad al-Normandy, meaning from Normandy; or Maxime Hauchard, Abou Abdallah Al-Faransi, from France, celebrated in caliphal strategic communications for being a fearless and irreproachable hero.[18]

This fact, that the foreign caliphal soldier's territorial origin (*nisba*) is noted, is not insignificant: It affirms that "Amrik" and France are potentially the Caliphate's provinces. The young

Australian nicknamed in English, in ignorant derision, "Jihadi Jake" bears a very noble name in the Caliphate as the "father of the servant of God in Australia": Abou Abdallah al-Australi.[19] And so forth.[20]

This operation of renaming or identifying, coded in Arabo-Muslim culture,[21] affirms a symbolic takeover of territories yet to be conquered; it is systematic. Each foreign combatant re-marks new territory to be captured.

In other words, the rhetorical manipulation consists in sig-nifying that a terrorist act is not a prompt act of invasion; it is an act of takeover or of repossession.[22] Territory we think of as ours is not. We are strangers where we believe we are at home because this "at home" is infidel, immoral, criminal.

This countercharge is especially vehement in the case of those Caliphate partisans who come from societies nourished on benign consensualism with no ambitions to offer but a good-natured ma-terialism, like Australia[23] or, disturbingly, Canada—and we are dealing with converts here who, for example, answer to house-hold names like André Poulin, now turned into Abou Muslim, a combatant in the Caucasus, the hero of the propaganda film *Flames of War* in September 2014.[24]

The terrorist exists in order to persuade us that we must turn these "homes of ours" in the direction of the Caliphate and hitch our wagons to it. We are the criminals, not the partisan of the Caliphate who undertakes a beheading or knifes someone or guns someone down on a street in a Western city: The act of terror is there to inspire "a salutary fear" that will bring us to restore our territory to the path of righteousness.

THE MANTRA OF TERRITORY

If the Caliphate's bid for territory can be split into a tripartite strategy, it is that this complies with Koranic standards. In "The Opening," the Koran's canonic and nonchronological first sura, its eloquent prologue, the *Al-Fatiha*, to wit, in verses 6 and 7:

> Guide us (O Lord) on the Straight Path. The path of those upon whom Thou hast bestowed Thy bounties, not (the path) of those inflicted with Thy wrath, nor (of those) gone astray.

The five daily prayers are only valid if this sura is recited: It is the opening sura, operational and performative, daily. It reminds believers, five times a day, of the mental map of the territory of Islam, for whoever wishes may measure the words that God has spoken and that the Caliphate tirelessly repeats, like a mantra.

The opening sura delivers the key to the Caliphate's territorialization of humankind into three groups.

It delineates a mental map, for it designates three territorial movements by analogy with three key expressions:[25] first, a movement of return toward caliphal territories, holy lands, that assures Muslims of the "righteous path," a regular feature of the Caliphate's strategic communications, in short, emigration out of apostate territories (Saudi Arabia, Russia's Caucasus,

Kurdistan, Turkey, etc.) toward the lands of Islam; second, a violent movement that is a rejection of those against whom God is "incensed"—that is, Jews (this too is a constant in the communications materials); third, a movement of revolted flight away from territories that have "strayed,"[26] previously Christian or Christianized Western countries such as Spain, Southern Italy, the Balkans, together with a particularly poignant aspect of the *hegira*, the salutary emigration of women and of children (see chapter 7).[27]

The Caliphate is a territorial reality built out of this rhetoric, a physical and eloquent force that provides politics with a new formula. Instead of rhapsodizing the subtleties and professionalism of the Caliphate's strategic communications, we must reflect on what its devices are and what its dynamic is: the appearance of a language that transcends borders and turns our usual ways of talking politics on their heads.

Moreover, the terrorizing effect of a territorial and ideological political conception that erupts abruptly, aggressively bearing stupefying moral exigencies is not new: Is the Caliphate any more stunning than the French Republic was when it erupted out of the natural boundaries steadily set by the monarchy to annex whole territories in the name of abstract but weighty principles? Or than the nascent American Republic when it ravaged Native American territories in the name of Liberty and the right to happiness? For these two political innovations, the entire world was there to be republicanized—and to this day, this holds in the case of the official American foreign policy or national security discourse.

We must therefore begin by casting in this new mold our glossary concerning population movements and then cease to think of the emigration of French, German, British, and North American jihadists and the migration of refugees from across the Mediterranean and Eastern Europe as mere policing or humanitarian issues that have to be "managed" or made into emotional playthings. It is our mental map that needs to be redrawn and aligned to the mental map of terror cast onto the West by the Caliphate's vision of territorial capture.

THREE

"Terrorism," Linguistic Subversion

Wherein we examine the words we use to speak about terror and how we allow our vernacular languages to be subverted.

Terror is a powerful word. It entered the Western political glossary with the French Revolution. Let us reflect on it. In French it refers to the beating heart of the Great Revolution, the Terror, set up to extirpate the remnants of Old Europe's tyranny—the quality label borne by the Archangel of Terror himself, juvenile and idealistic revolutionary Saint-Just, in many ways not unlike the young men who today rally to the call of the Caliphate. But while the epithet "terrorist" was never applied to those who, like Robespierre, put in place the regime that went by that name, or to those who never themselves claimed it as an appellation, preferring "revolutionary" or "*enragés*" (the enraged ones, in the name of a sainted fury against oppression), the word *terrorist* was taken up quite casually by nineteenth-century Romantic anarchism.

But in 1920, when Trotsky evokes the Paris Commune, in response to critiques that Soviet communism is implementing the "Red Terror" in Russia, he celebrates terror as an adequate response to the White Terror. As far as he was concerned, this was not an anarchist or a romantic terror but a terror organized both strategically and tactically.[1] It was warfare. Terror that was not the act of individuals, often sacrificing themselves in the process, but an action by the masses and the Party, a class terror conferring a human sense and a sense of solidarity to one group's struggle against oppression—what Jean-Paul Sartre analyzes magisterially as "Fraternity-Terror."[2] Jihadism is a terrible fraternity.

In France, but also in other countries occupied by the Third Reich, it took the German Occupation for *terrorist* to take on a different meaning, the one given by the German enemy to the partisans, for no resistant would ever have claimed the term. In short, up until the current terrorism, and putting aside the Bolshevik instance, rarely could anyone call himself or herself a terrorist. The soldier of the Caliphate rarely refers to himself as a terrorist.[3]

The Caliphate, however, in a rhetorical reversion, has appropriated the insult (the way African-Americans might at times call each other *nigger*). The appropriation was carefully phased in.

The caliphal periodical in German was the first to make the evocative (in Germany) term *legion* its own: "ISIS has assembled a multi-ethnic army, a quasi–Foreign Legion to protect its territory."[4] In January 2015, the term *terrorist* (in the English issue) was used as a citation by the enemy, in quotation marks. And, starting in April 2015, *terrorist* was finally appropriated and glorified in an expression that instantly modified its tenor, *Soldiers of Terror,* where *soldier* is the key term.[5] This requalification is crucial.

You Say "Terrorist"? What Exactly Do You Mean?

Let us linger on this process of (re)-qualifying a denomination.

On the one hand, to name falls under the verbal management of the other and should always be the first rhetorical action in war: One must name the enemy, and the name must stick. The same goes in times of peace and reconciliation: Europeans (except perhaps the British) no longer say "German" but "Nazi" atrocities, and the expression "the liberation" of Germany, not its "defeat," was used by some media during the 2015 celebration of the victory of May 1945.[6]

On the other hand, as with the transformation of "terrorist" into "soldier of terror," a name never comes alone, it sets off qualifications or re-qualifications.

A substantive needs a qualifier. Our rhetorical existence is an assemblage of names and of qualifiers. A qualifying adjective brings a qualification because it allows species to be distinguished from one another ("a large apartment," "a cool car," etc.). Such is the use of the adjective in practical life; it serves to illustrate that things are in the same category, yet different. Qualifications open a rhetorical field of permutations: Therefore, to go back to *Soldiers of Terror,* saying "soldier of terror" is like saying "a war of terror," so it is no longer simply saying "terrorist" and sending the ball back into the court of those who use it as an insult.

With caliphal terrorism, the qualification becomes panic, a panic that underscores our increasing inability to name the phenomenon.

DRIFT OF QUALIFIERS

Where the "terrorist" theme is concerned, a plethora of qualifying labels exists for want of our having mastered substantives, a linguistic panic that is reflective of a political panic.

Starting with the acronym: Although we know the importance of labels as a tool for mobilizing attention in marketing,[7] in the chaos of the counterattack glossary, a flotsam of acronyms has emerged that disperses the attention: "ISIS," which means what exactly? *Islamic State of Iraq and al-Sham,* or, for the "S," *and Syria?* (opinions vary, as in, even if *Sham* is what the S stands for, according to certain instant philologists, *Sham* is the real name of Syria, etc.), "ISIL" (the official United Nations and U.S. State Department version).[8] And now *Daesch,* or *Daish,* lifted from a French coinage, *Daech.*

Next come the appellations by Arabization of language with forms that refer to nothing known in our linguistic code: "Daesh" (supposedly a transcription of the unpronounceable and Ubu-esque Arabic phrase *Dawlat al-Islāmiyya fī al-Irāq wa s-Shām*, but is also, according to certain Arabic anti–Islamic State sites, a derisive acronym).[9]

Lastly, there are bizarre verbal inventions: An Australian prime minister spoke of the "death cult Daesh,"[10] and the round of paraphrases and euphemisms such as "the so-called Islamic State or IS," "the group calling itself the Islamic State," "the jihadist group IS," or simply "IS"—which, for its part, poses the problem clearly and delivers the key to this rhetorical panic of qualifiers.[11]

Because with IS, is the qualifier "Islamic" or "Islamist"? A blunder and a hurdle in the panic of qualifiers. The suppressed qualifier, "Islamic," carefully avoided by politicians and the media, springs forth, not unlike the psychoanalytical return of the repressed. "IS," "Islamic State," the media and the politicians repeat. No one says "Islamist State." The key adjective is, in fact, resisting this rhetorical panic: "Islamic." And yet the public discourse makes a virtue of distinguishing those who are good, the "Islamic," from the evil ones, the "Islamists." But the Caliphate is resolutely termed "Islamic."

It is our panicked obsession to say "terrorist" that is the source of the trouble and leads us to say "Islamic" instead of "Islamist." Why is that?

The reason is that, since we have not mastered the substantive, we make up for it with qualifying adjectives or qualifiers that, in turn, slip from our grip, and we find we are using the very term we wish to repress in official and political discourse: "Islamic." The "terrorist" is an "Islamic terrorist," he is Islamic, and the Caliphate therefore incarnates "Islamic terrorism." It is the Islamic State. The one and only. The Caliphate has cause to celebrate.

A symbolic swap occurred while we were focused on "terrorist": Our naming code let "Islamic" in. We have been caught out.

We are incapable of naming terrorism because from the outset, in our rhetoric of naming, we made a poor choice, what can be called (with reference to the most recent historical period of "terror" in Europe, pre-Caliphate), a "German" choice: Not unlike the Occupiers of 1940–44, Europeans refuse to do two things. On the one hand, to accept that "terrorists" are militants, soldiers, combatants, not unlike Dutch, French, Belgian, Polish guerrillas who were called "terrorists" by Germans but called themselves "resistants." Jihadists operating in Europe portray themselves as resistants against the iniquitous, in their opinion, laws of Europe that "terrorize" them. Why not refer to them as such: "partisans" or "guerrillas" when they operate on European or American soil, "soldiers" when they operate in the Middle East? On the other hand, we have refused to identify them by employing the qualifier they themselves use and that we apply to their State, "Islamic."

The terms of the conflict are getting away from us. We have become linguistically impotent.

THE TERMS OF THE CONFLICT

This error in naming lets the Caliphate control how we speak of it. We need only say "soldier" and "partisan" for there to be a coincidence of words and things and leave aside the rhetorical effects of *terrorist*, in the term's worst sense. But this would also mean facing the reality of facts: war, and civil war. This aligning of words and facts would be the mark of political voluntarism that the state alone can put into play.

The Caliphate is therefore furnishing the terms of the conflict: When we say "Islamist terrorist," it immediately allows it to signal—and the Caliphate's propaganda runs with this—that in our countries, there are, in effect, false Muslims, apostates, and renegades, those we call "Islamic" in order not to call them "Islamist" and ruffle their feathers (the *fatwa* of death that weighs on renegades, should they fail to find the right path, does not appear, on the other hand, to preoccupy either their imams or the police).

Paradoxically, by saying "Islamic" for the Caliphate, we are highlighting what the Caliphate declares: that Muslims outside Islam, in Europe, are false Muslims since they accept that infidels should decide what is and is not Islamic.

This is the constant gaffe of the political class, to declare, out of oratorical prudence, that this is not the true Islam. How can an impious individual designate himself theological advisor and pronounce the law, and hence issue, for that is the term, a *fatwa?* It is risible, but it is naive and counterproductive.

We, in fact, are affirming what the Caliphate's propaganda

wants us to affirm, that Muslims living outside Islam are also the reason for the terrorism there and that they must be shown the true path, that of the Caliphate. The Caliphate recruits in Europe because that is where the work of "rectification"—as Mao would have put it regarding, say, intellectuals—of restoring to the purity of faith, is needed. By definition, it is not needed on the Caliphate's territory; outside its territory it is imperative.

The Parasitic Koranization of Language

Any language functions on the basis of codes of recognition. This incapacity to name, therefore, generates a second panic malfunction in the vocabulary: The (French) media rush to put an accent on *islam, jihad,* or *djihad,*[12] *sharia* or *shari'a;* on the web *khilafat* is frequently used for Caliphate;[13] and, in English, the hitherto unheard-of *u* is added in *Allah(u) akbar*—in short, as a result of the linguistic panic, the rush to imitate what is increasingly turning into a parasitic language inside our codes of speech. Entrenching the parasitizing of our language are sounds that refer to nothing within our linguistic code: Does one pronounce *i'a* in *Shari'a* or the macron on *Allāh?* What is it? These signs mean literally nothing to everyday users of English, French, or German, as they cannot be recognized, hence do not make sense. Yet the media are awash with them. This is a form of parasite language that transforms what we know into something foreign and intimidating. Exoticism in everyday use of language is fine, if restricted to cookbooks. When life is at stake, we had better watch out.

What is unfolding, in reality, is the transformation of a known, recognizable, and standard glossary by a parasite language that is taking over our linguistic bearings and finding a footing inside our community of discourse (see chapter 11).

This is how, to quote Faye, "the implicit organization of a quasi-language"[14] is constituted: A sub-language subverts the common language by introducing forms of expression into it that take root and become natural. The language that French or English soldiers of the Caliphate use on social networks, that they read in their periodicals and hear in videos or in the course of sermons and cell meetings is acceptable in their discourse community, but where our discourse community goes, it is a parasitic language.

This parasitic language is an aspect of the Koranization of Western public discourse in lockstep with the Koranization of political discourse in the Caliphate's periodicals, itself a voluntary spin on the Koranization of politics under the first Caliphate.[15] The entire glossary of this parasitic language has created its own language within English or French, a parasitic quasi-language. Ironically, one need only compare the florid and proper French (not a single *Allah*) of the *Recueil d'avis juridiques* by the European Council on *fatwas* (2002), written by the Muslim Brotherhood,[16] to the increasingly incomprehensible language French media use when they talk about caliphal terrorism to grasp that the rhetorical codes are controlled by the adversary, who, with our own complicity, is imposing a parasitic language on the

French public that is gradually occupying the rhetorical and the political terrain: a subversive language spoken by some Francophones and French who have joined the Caliphate, an entire range of new expressions—witness the Caliphate's French publication *Dâr al-Islâm*. France is mentioned here, as it has been the prime target in recent years. But it applies to English as well and is likely to increase in intensity if the Caliphate designates North America as the next territorial target of choice for guerrilla warfare. Changes in language precede action on the ground.

This subversion of language has a corollary: It makes us speak and listen to counter-truths and absurdities.

Here is a scene of rhetorical idiocy: A jihadist is stopped, a neighbor is interrogated, and you hear the neighbor state that "he was a young man that never got into any trouble."

The problem here is this: The neighbor is speaking this "sub-language" that, underneath language, makes us say all kinds of nonsense by imposing an unconscious norm. The neighbor has become incapable of thinking while speaking. We listen to an English Muslim quite calmly asserting that the infamous jihadi John was a "beautiful young man," a really good guy, and we read that his comrade Maxime Hauchard was a quiet young man,[17] expressions that the media, in a complete monophony, repeat unquestioningly. To cite them from A to Z is itself to speak the language of *jihad*.

This laxity is cowardice. Our social passion for the respect of others runs the risk of making us infantile in expressing judgment. The weakening of our rhetorical control is spreading to an inability that characterizes our everyday language, of naming what is atrocious and cruel and therefore of naming things: To say "he was a bit worrying" is already a linguistic misstep, it means you are "phobic." Our rhetorical codes have been disarmed.

How We Speak Falsely

The French state is no longer fulfilling its linguistic function. Representing the French language has always been, so to speak, the eminent domain of the French state. The French language is a state language; beginning with the royal *Ordonnance de Villers-Cotterêts* (1539), up through the banishment of regional languages by the Republic and encompassing recent state spelling regulations in schools, the state, in France, is the custodian and protector of the language. In the United States language does not reside with the federal government, although the question of the primacy of English as the indicial language of the nation flares up regularly. However, no Western culture is immune to a Koranization of its perceived or affirmed national idiom. And this carries consequences, first and foremost our ability to name who does what.

THE REFUSAL TO NAME

When we proceed to arrest nationals who have left to fight with the enemy, who have been accomplices in armed actions and, at times, in the slitting of throats, including on our national soil, why not simply state, whether military or civilian, that these are traitors and, if we are at war, as Western governments tell us we are, why not state they must receive the treatment reserved for traitors if they are American, German, British, or French nationals, as they are more often than not?[18]

In the case of the first Paris attacks, why not say, in fact, that the female police officer who purportedly provided assistance to the jihadist Coulibaly should be accused of treason? If the French are at war, and given that she is, moreover, a member of the military as gendarmes are, she should face surely the criminal penalty of life in prison and a fine of €750,000.[19] Abou Siyad al-Normandy is condemned to a one-year prison term of being an apologist for terrorism: If France is not at war (which is not what the government has been saying all along), then his treason still calls for thirty years of criminal detention and a fine of €450,000.[20]

What sort of prosecutorial restraint prevents the law from taking its course against American jihadists, whether they are combatants in the Middle East or guerrilla partisans on American soil, and have them charged with treason if they are American citizens? The U.S. Code is explicit in this regard: "Whoever, owing allegiance to the United States, levies war against them or adheres to their enemies, giving them aid and comfort within the United States or elsewhere, is guilty of treason and shall suffer death, or shall be imprisoned not less than five years and fined under this title but not less than $10,000; and shall be incapable of holding any office under the United States."[21]

This is not about what the law states, but about how the state chooses to say one thing in political debate ("a war of civilizations," "we are at war") and another through its repressive or judicial measures.[22] The state uses a doublespeak, and this doublespeak is all the more lethal because the Caliphate is direct, straightforward, to the point in waging war and naming it.

A state, it goes without saying, must play on a number of rhetorical registers. But what matters here is the rhetorical choice made by the state not to name the evidence. And the rhetorical servility of the media apparatus that relays what the state dishes out, without blinking and without truly wanting to name the actions of a police officer who commits treason, of the seemingly contrite returnee who does not get punished, of nice, quiet individuals who cross over to the enemy.[23] They are traitors.

It is surprising that in countries where the media are adept at dissecting every word, at questioning every expression, at splitting hairs about every talking point, at taking down a politician on the basis of a tweet, all this expertise is vitiated and silenced in the face of the very grave problem of naming acts of treason.

Therefore, we must take back control over codes of speech. Take back the rhetorical leadership in order to name terrorism. We can start by rejecting the complacent discourse of the media and the ready-made speech of state agencies.

A debate, in France, did take place, however, at the Assemblée Nationale about the reinstatement of something close enough to an indictment for treason, "national indignity," a crime hastily placed on the statute books in the immediate aftermath of World War II to punish those who had collaborated with Germany. The transcript of the debate, which is long, only uses the word *treason* twice and in the following argument:

> To denounce an individual as "guilty of high treason" in 1789, as "a traitor to the country" in 1793, or to charge him with the offense of "national indignity" in 1944, not only aimed to qualify the facts of which he was accused, but appeared as a means for the new powers to very strongly declare, with all the symbolic weight of the words selected, that the state itself would take care of those who inspired the greatest horror in the community and constituted the most serious threat against its existence and cohesion. In short, this was about an authority still in the throes of constituting itself establishing the idea that it was aware of the threat, that it saw it for what it was, and that it undertook by the tools that it would legally establish, to repress it.[24]

In other words: the terrorist danger, that according to the state endangers France to such a degree that the national army is currently deployed by the tens of thousands on the national soil, does not "inspire horror in the community," nor does it constitute "the most serious threat," since (according to our legislators) the state is not "in the constitution process." Note here the sophism. The experts consulted were all law professors, not a single philosopher who might have explained things from a different perspective. Such is the import of a parasitic sub-

language: It perverts the ends of justice and natural law by sub-
verting words.

What to do? We can begin, by simply no longer writing *Allah*
but writing "God" instead, to constrain the Caliphate's Islamic
propaganda to find another term, to employ a circumlocution,
to explain that by "God" they mean this and not that. And by
extending this linguistic strategy to everything that is parasitic
(see above). In short, by forcing those who are communications
strategists to make do with our language. Thus rendering their
task more difficult by maintaining, for our part, linguistic and
rhetorical confusion in the opposing camp.

Inversely, we must stop the panicked drift of words and employ the single term *caliphate*. The term is coded in European
languages, it belongs to a known glossary, it is party to a long
history about which we have some idea, even if we do not know
it in detail. The word brought about an object. The code has
reappeared. It is here to stay. We might as well use it, and only
it. Vis-à-vis our discourse community, it is enough to no longer
say "terrorist" but instead to say "guerrilla," "partisan," or "soldier," for the mirage to dissipate and the veil be torn on the
reality of this confrontation; for suddenly the public would be
constrained to employ normal, ordinary terms, a commonly ac-
cepted rhetorical code that, while making the "terrorists" lose
their exceptional character, would begin to reestablish the ordi-

nary norms of language: attack, defense, victory, defeat, battle, skirmish, reprisal, partisan, collaborator, prisoner, execution by firing squad, war crime, traitors. We would make the partisans and soldiers of the Caliphate adjust to the norm of our codes.

In the face of the Caliphate's strategic communications, this rhetorical strategy—to speak about the Caliphate and its militants, by refusing all Arabization and Koranization of our glossary—would implement all the suitable resources that standard English, French, German, Italian, and Spanish languages provide, including, in spite of everything, the resources provided both by our shared intellectual tradition and the Greco-Roman heritage of our legal and political ideas. Hence, speaking a language that is precise and exacting. A language that is armed.

It is by speaking our language, and only our language, that we will begin to regain control. By forcing the adversary, in its propaganda, to speak like us and not by consenting to speak like them. But we would also need, politically, to adopt this rhetorical courage, especially in the event of a territorial demise of the Caliphate, as its defeat should release the full force of its cyber propaganda, unmoored from combat on the ground and let loose on the terrain of ideas.

FOUR

Digital Caliphate

Let us imagine a scenario inspired by a surprising sentence from the French Renaissance essayist Montaigne. Having experienced the terror of the Wars of Religion in the Renaissance and confronted the conquest of (soon to be Latin) America by the Conquistadors, the terror waged on native cultures, and conversions at the end of a musket, he exclaimed: "Mechanical victories!" His argument was that in wishing to civilize, that is to say, to convert these idolatrous societies to the true faith, Europe had destroyed them without improving their people in any way. These were mechanical victories obtained by superior technology, in the absence of arguments. A mechanical terror.

So let us imagine a Caliphate, under the first restored caliph or his successor, that with its military sophistication on the ground, the efficiency of its guerrillas abroad, or its communication strategies spreads to the Maghreb on its Atlantic shore,[1] seizes the lucrative South Algerian territories, and, circling NATO-ized Turkey, establishes itself in the Islamic Balkans ("what is left of the fortresses of Islam in Europe"),[2] destabilizes Italy and Spain by way of migratory fluxes,[3] and to the East, gains a foothold in the Caucasus,[4] overflows into India, which once belonged to Muslim Mughals,[5] and expands out toward southeast Asia.[6]

Such a geopolitical map is not science fiction. It is a foreseeable scenario. The Caliphate may be displaced territorially from its original core, but its dominos remain on the chessboard of its global strategy.[7]

Next, let us imagine that thirty years from now a Muslim Montaigne writes, with all the requisite oratorical precautions, about the triumph of his religion and the expansion of the Caliphate to the threshold of Europe and exclaims, "Mechanical victories!" And he draws this conclusion: The destruction of Western or Westernized societies that, while rich, varied, cultured and developed, were idolatrous and pagan and no doubt cunning, violent, and immoral in the wars they waged (not unlike those Montaigne saw waged against the Aztecs and the Incas in his own time), was a consequence of the "mechanical" superiority of the terror waged by the Caliphate, not a consequence of a moral triumph brought about by the innate superiority of Islamic culture (just as, after the conquest of Latin America, the Spaniards were able, oblivious of war technology, to assert the "natural" superiority of Christian civilization).

Why this fiction?

To drive home the fact that if, on the surface, the "mechanics" are on the side of Westerners who dispose of massive and "specialized"[8] armament, in reality it is the Caliphate that has the "mechanical" advantage by the standards of our own ideology and our fervor for the digital.[9]

The Internet Utensil

The Caliphate can boast a mechanical advantage in the sense that jihadists control the digital weapons of terror better than anyone has before them. We are not, in the twenty-first century, dealing with the muskets, armor, or horses of conquistadors but the Internet,[10] which is an immense machine, an "inspired" e-mechanics.[11]

The Caliphate has strategic communication agencies, among them one that targets foreign countries, the Al-Hayat Media Center (and the Al-Furqan Foundation for Media Production), which is run by a capable team,[12] but their performance is not merely technical.

It is fed by our devotion to the communications superiority of electronic media, and in particular by our belief in the cognitive primacy of visual media—a "mechanical" illusion.

The strength of the Caliphate's propaganda is its use of our digital fervor, our certitude that the Internet and digital technology is ours and that we control it. And yet, after two world wars, we ought to know that technology has no moral values. It is that for which it is used. We believe that the Internet's mechanics, the perverse vanity of Facebook, the catch-all of YouTube, and the cozy comfort of social networks and secure messaging are in their essence "good," because we invented them. But all of these are digital utensils, and the Caliphate uses them.

The great sophistry that is the Internet is a lure of our own making, it assures and reassures us that we are in control of the virtual world, its psycho-neurological effects, and that this control is the sign, the proof, of our greater technical—even moral—superiority.

This auto-persuasion would work to our advantage were we to accept completely what the mechanics of the digital tool, like all mechanics, imply: the non-existence of God, a radical materialism, that is to say the conscious affirmation that the world can be boiled down to role playing and that with the Internet, given its rhetorical capacity for illusion and for the virtual, we have at last eliminated God.

But few among us have the courage of this conviction, that is, the courage to state that all is merely mechanics and matter. The Caliphate, therefore, is playing both with our conviction that this mechanics is ours, that we understand it best, and with our inability to concede the truth that our daily materialism demands: to acknowledge an effective materialism. It is doubtful that the USSR would have approached the question of the Caliphate as we are doing.

It is in this gap that the digital prowess of the Caliphate resides, in our illusion that this propaganda is powerful because it functions digitally, because it admits, claims, celebrates that it is only employing the Internet and its mechanics in order to accomplish the triumph of a thing that, paradoxically, to us, seems surprising, archaic, primitive, "medieval": the active and forthright defense of God.

Short of acknowledging the materialism that, after all, is the underpinning of our way of life, we are trapped between our fascination with all things digital and our opinion that the Caliphate is backward, savage, medieval. How can a backward regime be hypermodern?

Caught short, fascinated by what is a paradoxical form, we fall back on the last resort in counterattacks: the imitation of the means of terror—since we can neither oppose terror with terror nor oppose a militant, and military, Islam with a superior or equivalent belief—and, for the time being, military might, which, in this case, would call for accepting a war without mercy, which we are unwilling to countenance (see chapter 13).

But how do we use digital tools for the counterattack?

The Stop-Jihadism Video, or the Blunder

We answer the Caliphate's digital rhetoric with a poor imitation.

A compelling example is the first anti-jihad video produced by the communications wing of those fighting terrorism in France.[13] It was a remarkably sophisticated attempt at turning the tables on the enemy, and it failed. To date it does not seem that Western counter-messaging agencies have drawn any lessons from this failure. Budgets have increased; communication wisdom has not.

The video lasts 1 minute 50 seconds. The optimal length for a video of that sort is 3 minutes. The video is structured as follows: a section that is a teaser, 23 seconds; four argumentation segments composed of a first message, a sub-video, a final message, each lasting 19 seconds; and a concluding message, 6 seconds; then closing with the logos and institutional links, 5 seconds.

In the introductory segment a sentence is the first problem: The person watching the video is put in the position of someone, "a young man," surfing the web looking for information about jihad—it looks like Facebook. Gradually, in the course of the video, the images turn increasingly crude, thus imitating an ever more focused search by the fictitious Internet user, culminating in a beheading (at 0′07″). At 0′14″, the person navigating to the point of no return sees himself contacted directly by an audio signal that announces the arrival of a message: "uv' got friends there bang bang amped to hook you up."

First sticking point: Whom is this video addressing? Don't forget, although the video is fictitious, it has nevertheless been posted so that a young person surfing the Internet can come across it and take it to be a real video for a few seconds, just long enough to trigger the dissuasive argument. The goal is to avoid recruitment; in the event of a real recruitment situation, this video, already seen, should provoke a critical reaction. If all that the young person is seeking is to obtain information, the same goal will be attained.

The problem, however, of the person targeted (the young man) is that he will cross over from credulous receptor to critical receptor only if all of the elements for such a shift of status are in place.

The first element in play is the language used by the fictitious sender of the message (the one who, in the video, messages the young man, as he might in a real situation). With no images, without a "face," it is through language and language alone that the existence of the sender (a presumed recruiter) makes itself known: His credibility is based on this alone. The young person navigating the Internet and coming across this video must recognize the true language of recruiters with whom he may have had exchanges in the sentence cited or, after seeing the clip, if and when he is later approached by a recruiter, the same operation of "recognition" must be triggered.

There is, in linguistics, a fundamental distinction between "language" (*langue*) and "speech" (*parole*): A jihadi language exists, a "caliphal" language, with key terms, codes, phrases, a general rhetoric. Alongside it jihadist speeches exist that vary from group to group, practically from individual to individual (according to their level of education, age, their dexterity on the Internet), making intelligence work complicated: This citation is a made-up example. *Langue* and *parole* must not be confused.

Until now, with the parade of images, messages, posts, etc. in the course of the fictitious search undertaken by the individual who is the subject of this video, we were in jihadist language, the universal rhetoric of jihad. With the quote, speech is exercised, in other words, individual expression: A real person (the sender of the message) is supposedly addressing the recipient, the "young man," directly, in a personal mode.

And this is the first mistake: The quote is too much, "uv', amped, hook you up." Let us not forget that the video is targeting young people in the *mise en scène* of its first segment. If you are the young man and are reading the quote, does your speech match that of the fictitious recruiter—himself imitating the supposed speech of the young person? Probably not.

The scenario would be more effective if the fictitious recruiter, on the contrary, employed a disjunctive language, thus eliciting the young person's attention in the quest for recruitment, that is to say, an elevated, noble, sacral, caliphal language, instead of parodying the scrambled language of an imaginary "young man."

At the start of the first segment, "-12" appears on screen. This is not intended for viewers under twelve years of age. Imagine being the target audience for this video and abruptly seeing the "-12": Do you shut down your screen?

A serious semiotic hitch: at 0′07″, when the violent image of a beheading appears (at the time this video appeared, it was impossible to view this in the French media), there is no mention of the "-12." So (sticking to the fictional scenario in which the antiterrorism services are courting me as a potential jihadist) I could, at age eleven, watch an image that most adults have trouble finding and would find difficult to watch even if they could find it, given how nauseating it is: Me, at age eleven, I can watch a combatant of the Caliphate slit the throat of a prisoner. Me, at eleven, I am one of the privileged. All it takes is to watch this video. To put it mildly, this is strange: How is a person under twelve (-12) less susceptible than a person over twelve (+12)? The video has tied itself into knots.

In any case, the semiotic snafu is serious: The victim in the video is not, on the strength of the evidence, a Syrian. The series of four segments bases its dissuasive argument on the fact that it is the Syrians who are the real victims of the Caliphate: The young potential jihadist will see images (censored or made opaque, images of crucifixions of headless bodies, etc. from here on out) of local victims, Syrians to whose aid the young man will supposedly wish to come by turning himself into a militant for the Caliphate. If, as the fiction of this video assumes, the young man is an agile practitioner of all things Internet, then the cognitive process at work in the course of his web navigation, which consists of an accumulation of sensations, of visual memory magnified, would have signaled to him that something was off already.

The wish to imitate the language of the Caliphate, verbal and iconic, has led us to an accumulation of errors of judgment.

Aestheticizing Terrorism

But it gets worse: We have chosen to aestheticize the enemy in four sequences, each 19 seconds long and each using the same three-part structure.

First a message in golden letters, its style direct (example, at 0′24″: "Sacrifice yourself at our side, you will be defending a just cause") prefaced by a declarative (example, same sequence: "They tell you:"), both superimposed over a video showing the militants of the Caliphate in immaculate black combat uniforms standing before a Muslim crowd that itself stands out against a golden yellow backdrop. We don't know if the video is real, or if it is a montage produced by the strategic communications team, but if it is a montage—which it probably is—they should be congratulated for conferring such beauty to evil.

Suddenly, at 0′25″, a discordant audio interference shatters the beautiful litany of oriental chanting (soundtrack) and the picture turns black and white, a dirty grey, and a very quick message flashes three times over the execution videos before freezing with (soundtrack) a sinister tolling of bells (from 0′34″ to 0′43″): "In reality, you will discover hell on earth and you will die alone, far from home."

This is an absurd use of what is referred to as the phatic function (which ensures that communication is functioning correctly, as in "Hello, can you hear me?"): One wonders about the irritating flashing message on top of the rupturing effect of the grey images that follow the effect in black and gold and on top of the soundtrack. This flashing is a signal, and this kind of signal, in message theory, is called the phatic function. But the brutal interruption of the chanting (a *nasheed*) with untimely static is a signal to the young person who is watching and listening that there is actually a foreign presence, a "parasite" to be exact, a hostility, a third party who is eavesdropping.

The triple rupture (sound, color, message) is meant to recall the young person to salutary reality, but the reality that suddenly shatters the perceptive flow indicates that he is being tracked, observed, that he is in hostile surroundings.

There may have been another strategy for interrupting both the beauty of the images and the beauty of the chanting. But the communications people, having chosen to aestheticize the enemy, were forced into this choice and were therefore forced to resolve the sequence as they set it up: parasite, grey image, the grey tolling of the bell. A counter-use of the phatic function.

If first impressions are what counts, it is almost certain that the youth over the age of twelve who is supposed to watch the counterterrorism video, taking it for a jihadist video (for this is the goal and conceit of the video), is saying to himself, "I was into it at first, but man, real drag, fucking coppers . . ." (an attempt at sticking to the codes of speech attributed to him by those running this program).

WHY THE BLUNDER?

The makers of the video lost sight of the second lesson of semiotics, even though it is so endlessly rehashed in every communications course dating back to Barthes's earliest work, to wit, that an image as a verbal declaration functions on two axes: a horizontal axis (the chronological sequence of words and shots) and a vertical axis (how each word or shot is the result of a selection or of a permutation in the same paradigm or semantic category; for example "dough" with "money").

As a result, an image functions on two axes: It is a moment in a film, a shot, the one the person—the young man tempted to join jihadist militants—freezes with a click of his mouse (the film's flow of images becomes this image); and an image is also a possibility for reordering the one image with what is no longer seen, what has disappeared because of the freezing of the one image. In actual fact, when I, as the young man, look at this grey and sad picture where I am being told "you will die alone" as a church bell is still tolling in my ear, I instantly connect this with that other sumptuous video I discovered while surfing YouTube and think, "That's where real life is! That's where the beauty of the world is! That's where there's magic to be found! Not here."

The strategic communications team appears to have not pondered the effects of such permutations. They appear to have thought only about the linear nature of the pictures, sounds, and slogans, the banal horizontal axis of communication stringing one image after another.

They have also peppered their film with other gaffes here and there; for example, in the third segment (at 1′16″) the supposedly dissuasive message has been inserted inside a cross. First the church bell, now the cross. Lacan said that the unconscious, the *Unbewusst*, is the unblunder: the blunder one does not see. These Christian symbols are the perfect example.

The video's creators are therefore guilty of incompetently handling the intellectual tools of their trade, such as the operative distinctions between sender and recipient, the tension between language and speech, the delicate balance of the axes of language. They are guilty of aestheticizing the adversary, of succumbing to embellishment; a video like this is war pursued by other means, not a potential Oscar nominee. They are guilty for not having questioned themselves as to what it is that attracts, what it is that engages, what it is that fills a young person tempted by jihadist militants with such enthusiasm: A rhetorician would have gladly reminded them that a message is persuasive only if it targets its audience at a precise given time and in a given context. Rhetoric holds that impact is calibrated according to three criteria: pure information, emotional triggers, a desire to communicate around values.

IMBECILES NEED NOT APPLY

But the fundamental flaw of this video, clearly sprung from the political doxa (that is, the governmental rationale that is running it by remote control) is its refusal to view jihadism as other than a pathology afflicting imbeciles.[14]

Aware as we are now of the sophistication of these videos, we should acknowledge that periodicals like *Dâr al-Islâm* in French, or *Dābiq* in English, strive specifically to target educated, intelligent young people, the beneficiaries of a cultural and material capital, attentive readers looking for a well-structured argument and carefully developed ideas (*Dābiq* no. 7 is 83 pages long): Among many others there are the three English high school girls who went over to the Caliphate, as well as Mohammed Emwazi, the mediatized haranguer of the throat-slittings with a degree in computer science,[15] and the young Australian hospital doctor who went to practice his profession in the place his convictions demanded he go.[16]

By contrast, the secret service video is addressed to imbeciles and ignoramuses.[17] The Caliphate's propaganda[18] is aimed at smart individuals who, moreover, have a thoughtfully considered desire for heroism and self-sacrifice.[19] One need only read their messages on social media[20] or the letters of conversion by the two young militants Jake Bilardi[21] and Elton Ibrahim Simpson, the Texan terrorist,[22] to fathom the gulf that separates them from the idiotic web surfers conceived by counterpropaganda. These young men are experiencing personal epiphanies. The English terrorists Adebolajo and Adebowale were also middle-class, well educated, and, on the face of it, unlikely to be vulnerable. It is possible that if the "Catholic" terrorist McVeigh, responsible for the Oklahoma City bombing of 1995 (168 dead; he was executed in 2001), were alive today he would have converted to Islam and joined the Caliphate— as implied by one of his writings in prison in which he denounced the invasion of Iraq. These are personal itineraries which censored accounts (see chapter 6) fail to portray, and spiritual journeys for which publications from the Caliphate's strategic communications agencies act as confirmation of intensely personal conversions.

A Rhetorical Asymmetry

Therefore, our rhetorical posture in the face of the Caliphate is asymmetrical.

HAVE WE TURNED INTO IDIOTS?

One does not respond to the incineration of a pilot by crying out "vengeance will be extraordinary"; in the Jordanian case, in contrast, the response consists of executing convicts previously found guilty, as though the application of a sentence previously handed down by the judiciary were vengeance.

One does not combat recruitment by dropping leaflets from an airplane as in the time of the trenches, comic book style to boot.[23]

One does not respond to films of throat-slittings by cutting a video here and there so as not to offend the public, in short, by symbolically killing victims or martyrs a second time, by refusing to let their true torment be known to one and all: It is a mistake to respond to a montage with another montage.

Have we turned into idiots? (An idiot in the true sense is one who gets trapped in his or her own idiom, world, language.)

No, of course not. We have simply placed ourselves in an asymmetrical posture.

PROPAGANDA AND DIVERSION

Fascinated as we are by the mirror of our addiction to e-communication, we fail to see that these videos are "tabloid" videos: They play with our sensations. While behind the mirror, direct recruitment takes place, territory is conquered, and the notorious victory over "hearts and minds," so dear to every theoretician of counter-insurgency strategy, is achieved; but it is not ours, the Caliphate is winning hearts and minds over to its cause, and by the thousands. If politics is a "calling," a "vocation," the political calling here is stacked on the side of the Caliphate.[24]

Where social networks are concerned, we now know that the Twitter accounts of jihadist soldiers of Western extraction are not significant sources of recruitment.[25] These are necessarily brief words, from apologists and, very infrequently, from the soldiers of the Caliph speaking about victims that have been executed. They do, on the other hand, celebrate heroes and exemplary militants, the glorification of martyrs and fraternity in combat. These brief exchanges are not acts of propaganda: They correspond to no strategic communication "design."[26]

On the other hand, it is now acknowledged that out-of-network recruitment is far more prevalent and that by closing accounts or applying heavy surveillance, we are in fact forcing the actors underground, forcing them to move into the shadows and melt into the background, to move outside of social networks. When the three English high school students left for the Caliphate, the father of one of them immediately launched a diatribe against the English government, its schools, and marginalization. It turned out, however, that it was he who had incited his daughter to join *jihad*: "Society" was not to blame for persuading her, it was his words that did it.

The videos and periodicals that counterpropaganda has rushed to respond to in a show of "doing something" modern and e-mechanical are therefore partly subterfuges and diversions, masking the operation on the ground and in the shadows—and partly the assemblage of a library that, in the spirit of the Caliphate, will be added to the spoken words and deeds of warring Islam, from its initial conquest of Damascus fourteen hundred years ago. Dazzling diversionary maneuvers that put us in an asymmetrical posture.

A stocktaking indeed reveals an asymmetry between the posture of the Caliphate's strategic communications and the West's posture of counter-strategy. The standard of a stratcomm campaign evolves from the clarification of objectives until final evaluation, with the identification of targets along the way. Clearly, nothing of the kind is in place on our side.

Put differently, the Caliphate, in the e-mechanics of the Internet, is going for quality, we are going for quantity. It is banking on heroism, we are banking on prevention. It is banking on transcendental soaring, we are banking on the white picket fence. It is banking on transcendence, we are banking on middle-class consumerism. It is banking on heroic journeys, we are banking on values. We want to "give-ourselves-the-means-to," the Caliphate is giving itself the ends.

It is time to become creative instead of pinning all our hopes on "mechanical victories."

FIVE

Strongspeak vs. Weakspeak

Speaking establishes a power dynamic.

Why does jihadist or caliphal speech inherently have such power to appeal, an attraction made material in enthusiastic conversions? And why does it provoke in its adversary only sarcasm, invective, or morbid fascination tinged with envy?

Why are we weak in the face of this force?

To understand the operation of a power dynamic informed by speech such as that of the Caliphate, it behooves us to undertake a two-pronged review of this question of speech as a mediator between the strong and the weak. This question has come up from the earliest instances of political persuasion. It hinges on two foundational scenes.

The Rhetorical Ultimatum

Long ago, when the Athenians were the dominant power in the West, they were keen on debate and rhetoric—the exact definition of democracy being a society organized through political debate, with Aristotle's *Rhetoric* as its manual. But in their relations with foreign powers both Asian and Greek, the Athenians acted differently. They employed a two-pronged rhetoric.

Vis-à-vis the Persians, the great power of the Orient and Asia—in many respects the "terrifiers" of the day—they maintained that these "barbarians" were characterized by their incapacity for political dialogue (for they did not speak Greek); and they remained submissive when faced with despotism, murmuring their obedience. As such, the Persians were incapable of "politics." The Athenians, expanding on Herodotus, added: "Of course an Asian barbarian can come over here, leave behind his colorful dress, trim his kinky beard, adopt our plain clothes and our manners, stop bleating, and learn to manipulate our language with some sophistication, but he will continue to think like a barbarian." And concluded: "Beware: the principal characteristic of the barbarian or immigrant is his ability to imitate us. Our weakness is that we forget this conjuring trick. Hence, against the Persians, war to the death, and no admiration for a people incapable of politics but skilled in mimicry."[1]

Vis-à-vis other Greek cities, Athenians, unable to refute their rhetorical capabilities, since they too were Greeks, made a different use of oratory and political speech: They did not hesitate to inform the cities they wished to annex that along with their army they had brought two goddesses, Force and Persuasion.[2] They set siege outside the ramparts and sent ambassadors to deliver more or less the following speech:

> Where we come from, among us, democratic dialogue and the free exchange of opinions are desirable, but not so with you, no, because you are not us. But being Greeks, like us, you want to discuss your surrender or your destruction among yourselves. We are going to allow you to debate this choice democratically among yourselves, because as Greeks you are rational and capable of a political decision made together. It is up to you to decide whether you should yield to Persuasion's argument that the weak must cede to Force; it is for you to discuss among yourselves and choose, argue it out, to see if your choice is to be destroyed in the derisive name of what you call honor, your identity, your culture, and all that will no longer exist when we have reduced you to nothing. Or whether to submit and stay alive and add your cultural acquisitions and your wealth to our empire. Discuss it, reach a common decision. It is up to you to choose between perishing through Force or accepting through Persuasion that the weak always submit to the law of the more powerful.

This, then, is the way that Athenians conceived of international power relations. Toward barbarians: a battle to the death if conflict was necessary. Toward Greeks: The weaker must bend, but they are given the possibility of debating among themselves, though not for long, the question of how to make the people accept or refuse a political decision.

This is an ultimatum that makes the weakest responsible

for the reasons of a choice imposed by the strongest. Force expresses itself and leaves Persuasion the time to do its work so that those who must die or submit may find justification and explanations. They become the bearers of rhetorical responsibility.

This foundational backdrop armed relations between European states until the First World War; the Greek episode described was known, cited, and used. It was a reference for statesmen, who in the old days were also men of Letters. And the example served them as an argument at the negotiating table.

The Dialogue-Obsession

Ever since the League of Nations, dialogue between states has been presented at the very least (and in its practical application) as a remedy against the use of force, and at best (in its ideal form) as an antidote to war.

Before the League of Nations, international political dialogue, or diplomacy, was undertaken to temporize, to delude, to scheme. Force led Persuasion.

For the last century, then, things would appear to have changed. Dialogue is no longer a lubricant: It is the fuel that ensures the functioning of all political management machines established in the intervening years (the United Nations, the EU, the non-aligned nations movement, and even the defunct Comintern, the many international organizations, a worldwide panoply of NGOs, etc.), for which they have been created piecemeal (this is equally true on the corporate side, from OPEC to the rating agencies). Persuasion, from now on, was seen to lead Force.

It is an illusion.

Westerners are behaving like Athenians: They impose their views through bombings and invasions while offering nonetheless a pretense of discussion. Since the carpet bombing of a recalcitrant Serbia by NATO, Force has taken the upper hand. But there is a difference that would have made the Athenians smile: We explain to the weakest (Serbia, Iraq, Libya) why we are morally obligated to take extreme measures. We surround ourselves with morality in debates at the United Nations. We arm ourselves with every possible oratorical precaution so as to remain within the framework that was established a century ago, that of an international politics whose principle is dialogue. We resort to Force in a display of morality, as if we have exhausted persuasive dialogue, and as soon as the deviant is forced to submit, we set up, as in devastated countries such as Iraq and Afghanistan, a whole system of persuasive propaganda, a stratcomm to "win hearts and minds."[3] We must show those we have mistreated that we did it for their own good. Humanitarian dialogue hinges on armed incursions.

For the last century, we have lived, or asserted that we must live, in a universe where everything can be resolved through dialogue while ensuring that we remain superior in force. Dialogue, or conversation as it is also paraphrased, has moved to first place in all of our political tracts and transactions, domestically as well as externally.

The Caliphate, however, has a different take on things.

In the eyes of the Caliphate, we miscreants are in the situation of the weak under attack by Athenians. We are inherently weak for we no longer conceive of politics as a whole where the key element is power and where speech is the element allowing the stronger party the following rhetorical strategy: to proclaim unilaterally the terms of an engagement; to leave a breach through which the weak can discuss the alternatives offered (submit or perish); and to give them a certain amount of time for a dialogue among themselves about the alternatives, time to take up their responsibilities. Listening to a terrorist haranguing "Obama" directly or threatening "France" with an ultimatum is akin to hearing an Athenian ambassador ordering a city to submit—except now it is the barbarian who speaks.

Hamstrung as we are by the ideology of salutary dialogue and the interference of morality in the use of force, we have lost the ability to adopt a different rhetorical posture.

Voicing Jihadism in France: The Power of the Appeal

What would this posture be? It would vary from political culture to political culture. In the case of France, the rhetorical posture should be "the appeal." The French ought to recognize the formula when they listen to the Caliph harangue his people for the simple reason that the appeal is a rhetorical key to French political culture. Since France remains a prime target of the Caliphate, as well as a prime supplier of insurgents, it is worth considering its case, how a previously strong political culture, measured by its rhetorical armament, disarms itself when confronted with a new, surging enemy rhetoric.

The last time French politics put dialogue aside, that is to say the capacity for exchanges about the crucial options of surviving or being put to death, was in 1940, with General de Gaulle's famous Appeal of June 18. Breaking strategically with the requisite political panderings of supply and demand, that is political transactions within the French establishment to settle an armistice, he broke ranks and became a de facto rebel (and was even labeled a traitor) by delivering, from London, an "appeal" to refuse dialogue with the enemy, with the legal government of France, and with those who agreed to lay down their arms. He addressed his fellow citizens directly, formulating a path to follow and placing before them a choice that rejected dialogue as a solution both personal (each "Free French" instantly became a traitor in the eyes of the legal, internationally recognized government and a terrorist in those of the enemy) and national (monarchists, communists, Catholics, Jews, people from the Colonial Empire responded instantly to his appeal). In substance, and such were the rhetorical posture and the armed words, de Gaulle's appeal said: Now, each and every one, accept your responsibilities and join me. Similar appeals had occurred before in French history and are quite specific to French political culture, at least since the Hundred Years' War and Saint Joan of Arc's appeal to "the Lord of Hosts" in defense of the realm. These are deep rhetorical markers of French political culture. Each Western political culture responds to extraordinary events that threaten its existence with different rhetorical tools and a different rhetorical posture, all tantamount to weaponizing words.

In this case, have the French heard an analogous appeal against the Caliphate? No. Coming from the Caliphate? Yes. It is a complete reversal of posture.

Indeed, the caliphal appeal is not different in the structure of its language and the effect it seeks from the Gaullist appeal: It is an appeal that sweeps aside transactions, accommodations, compromises, and negotiations and asserts the rhetoric of the appeal against the rhetoric of dialogue, commanding each person to choose, to take responsibility, to leave, and to join the source of the appeal.

The leaven for the rhetoric of the appeal is ethical: The appeal offers a new opening to the moral sense, one that leads to transcendence of the self, both territorially and mentally. Dialogue, in contrast, is not ethical, it is managerial: It puts no one face to face with moral responsibilities (contractual ones, yes); moreover, it offers shared responsibilities (presented as moral, to force adherence through guilt or fear); it points out a common place, a negotiating table or a human resources meeting, but not the trajectory, the way, the path.

It is clear that the caliphal appeal, in its stupefying novelty, breaks with the monotony of our culture of dialogue where everything is of equal value. At the opposite extreme, in a political culture that only functions by appeal, like South Africa under apartheid (the appeal to defend the white race, the appeal by opponents to defend the subjugated black population, the appeal to UN sanctions, the appeal to release Nelson Mandela, etc., an arresting and relentless succession of appeals that kept the anti-apartheid crusade at the forefront of international news for thirty years), it was the appearance, with Desmond Tutu, of the political necessity of dialogue between enemies that proved decisive: surprising everyone, by dint of which it acquired its ethical force and provoked a radical change and resulted in national reconciliation.[4]

The caliphal appeal, therefore, with the same strategic brutality as the Appeal of June 18, indicates that no, everything is not equally valid. This is the source of its persuasive power: This appeal offers something new, and the response is massive.[5]

Jihadism, the Caliphate, are trenchant. If "we are at war" with them, as the French government asserts, if terrorism is "intolerable," "unacceptable," there is nevertheless no ethical appeal forthcoming from the state, which, in France, has been the incarnation of sovereignty since 1789: If we are truly at war, and this war is against an intolerable and unacceptable politics, the state should call on the Nation to take up arms. There should be an "appeal."

On the contrary, facing an appeal that is ethical (because it transmits values that are transcendent), the appeal of the Caliphate, the French state has fallen back on crisis management, that is, back on the technologies of dialogue with "all concerned parties," with the support of police measures that harm civil liberties and, moreover, a continuous state of emergency, unique among Western democracies, that does damage to freedom of conscience. Unable to adopt a rhetorical posture, the French state attempts to "cure" jihadists through dialogue, prevention centers, psychological help, while using emergency measures that succeed only modestly in preventing terror attacks or in stopping the flow of young guerrillas joining the Caliphate.

On the other hand, all the biographical accounts of young jihadists who have responded to the appeal by the Caliphate confirm that the appeal of the Caliphate is the rebirth, in this tepid atmosphere of dialogue, of an annunciatory storm, the harbinger of a greater destiny. It has given a global "voice" to jihadism and given a voice to individuals. It had an appeal in the past, and it remains appealing.

Voicing Jihadism in America: The Jeremiad and the Martial Harangue

Turning now to what could be a rhetorical posture in the United States, it is striking that the caliphal utterances, broadcast across the nation, have revived two oratorical forms that have been long part of American political oratory: the religious jeremiad and the martial harangue.

Generally speaking, preaching serves to connect everyday personal life with divine grace and eternal life. However, in the gamut of predication, the genre of the jeremiad has always been more specific: Until the end of the nineteenth century it was most active at election time, when moral invective in the name of a will greater than human endeavors was applied to political choice at the ballot box. Having nearly vanished from the American political scene (except, on occasion, by a president after a national catastrophe), this transcendent form of speech has found now a new vehicle and vector: in jihadist videos, harangues, and periodicals. The American tradition of the religio-political jeremiad has been revived, but from the mouths of those who wish to destroy the American covenant.

Just as the French "appeal" has been turned against the French Republic, the American jeremiad has been retooled by the Caliphate against the American Republic.

Vanished too is that most political form, the martial harangue: a general addressing that segment of the nation in arms that is the army, or a chief addressing his battalion prior to an attack, acutely aware that war is politics pursued by other means and that in a national war, the leader on the ground is fulfilling a political role because those next to him are not mercenaries, they are citizens.[6] The troops were addressed before any decisive actions in the same way that citizens would be before an election.

Few have remarked that the caliph's second *urbi and orbi* harangue in May 2015 was not delivered on a Friday. Therefore, it was not a sermon, it was a military harangue, launched with precision on the day of the Ascension, the celebration of a martial messiah, of Jesus as the leader of Islamic armies:[7]

> We call upon you that you should leave the life of humiliation, disgrace, degradation, subordination, loss, emptiness, and poverty for a life of honor, respect, leadership, richness.[8]

In short, the caliphal appeal has restored three rhetorical forms to the universe of public speech that had enjoyed immense prestige in the past and had powerful ethical consequences: the appeal or proclamation to the people, the religious-political jeremiad, and the martial harangue at the moment of the supreme sacrifice.[9] Rhetorical genres for which France and America were illustrious. And of which nothing remains.

Bereft of a culture of proclamatory appeals, oblivious to the power of great sermons, disdainful of martial harangues, we have, rhetorically, atrophied.

A Lost Generation

Against the voluntarist idealism of our young jihadists, we propose dialogue and psychology: The counterpropaganda technicians and the "de-radicalization" assembly line make the pitiable but understandable mistake of thinking that these are precisely substitute values they are offering. But it is not possible to respond to the caliphal appeal, jeremiad, or martial call with a homologue of equal power unless values both precede and follow it. Do they precede it? Do they follow it?[10] No.

Oddly, and against our belief system, young Western jihadists are honoring a Western tradition, rushing to the rescue of an ideal. Young Americans who volunteered to form the Lafayette Flying Corps in World War I, young Europeans and Americans who joined the International Brigades during the Spanish Civil War, and before them young Catholics who took up arms to defend the Holy See at the time of Italian Unification preceded the thousands who have converted to Islam to defend the Caliphate. Under the long gaze of History they follow in hallowed footsteps, and that reality should challenge us. It serves no purpose to turn away from that fact. It is vain to refuse this evidence: We have a lost generation.

But what have we lost of ourselves to lose them this way?

SIX

The Jihadist Aesthetic

With this interrogation, we enter a new domain, the aesthetic power of the ideal. To the question: "What purpose does the Caliphate's online propaganda serve—its magnificent videos, its substantial publications fit for the covers of glossy magazines?" The answer erupts instantly: Seduction![1] This response is intuitive, but it is incorrect. It is a natural response on our part because it corresponds to what we think of as our relationship to the material world, structured by publicity and media, a world of communications and commodities. It is undoubtedly an aesthetic universe, but this aesthetic universe fabricates simulacra that make us forget that work alone never delivers full enjoyment of the material world, that our acquisitive powers are limited to exchanging this for that, driven by the "seduction" of marketing. Only capital, or theft, allows for the infinite pleasure

86

of amassing stuff. In other words, the amniotic lure of publicity induces us, or seduces us, to enjoy the simulacra of material acquisition, which are in fact defined and limited by the transient possession of substitutes. We live lives relative to perishable goals.

The explanation is therefore not that the Caliphate, in order to recruit or to terrorize, needs to have recourse, as though it were selling the latest crossover car model, to videos and hip publications. The Caliphate does not fall under marketing.[2] It is not a brand, and it does not produce franchises: Its "products" cannot be substituted by others, as in any market-driven economy. Its values are absolute, not relative and interchangeable. And that is where seduction and aesthetics gain ascendancy: the aesthetic power of the absolute.

On Influence

Contrary to what the security agencies apparently believe, and what strategic communications professionals evidently proclaim, terrorist videos are not sales pitches. Media commentators vaunt their sophistication, just as they are stunned by the vulgar savviness of the Russian television channel RT. A somewhat odd reaction among colleagues working in strategic communications remains their incapacity to conceive that communication is just a technology and that, as such, it is ideologically plastic and does not contain an inherently democratic destiny. It is a utensil.

It is telling too that the media do not perceive that starting with the first throat-slittings, and before anti-terrorist censorship, either a spontaneous censorship (virulent in England and in the United States, where any offending images, no matter to what degree, and for what group, are banned) or a formal code of ethics censorship (where the profession is regulated, self-regulated, or simply under orders) have prevented the public from seeing or downloading the videos: They were hard to find in their entirety, save by negotiating a labyrinth of filters and blocks. A potential recruit could not have immediate access to them on a cell phone.

The same phenomenon of withholding information can be observed in the Caliphate's luxurious multilingual publications, which are at times hard to access[3] or blocked by security agencies. When an ordinary media outlet cited the invective against "those dirty rats in France," showing the Eiffel tower, it was impossible to click on the photo and gain access to the periodical. The major media outlets refrain from propagating information. Some have gone as far as refusing to print the names of jihadists, still less post their images. In an ironic case of good intentions gone awry, it is an anti-Caliphate site that ensures the regular and stable publication of this material (in English).[4]

More telling still of our belief in simulacra is the fact that the media do not imagine that moral or legal censorship has been factored in by the Caliphate's stratcomm: Its producers, evidently, were not expecting media outlets in the West to relay the entirety of the videos. Their communications strategy had taken not only our obsession for Internet materials into account in advance but also our legal or ethical censorship.

Access on the part of the public who is supposed to be touched by this terrifying or terrorizing propaganda is limited, reduced to images made banal and carefully chosen by the media and swiftly swept into the torrents of news of every kind.

And sometimes, when the public is given the chance to see this or that video of throats being slit on some rogue website, a frequent reaction is: "No thanks, I don't want to, I can't watch 'that.'" We read and we see only what has been filtered by the media and, after the imposition of censorship, in the context of "national protective measures for combatting terrorist threats,"[5] only what is authorized by security agencies.

It also remains to be proven that a full disclosure of these images would provoke such scandal in the public opinion that a resistance movement would take shape. As it is, everyone carries on, going about their business, and a beheading becomes just one more fact in the mediatized amniotic bath in which we evolve. Very few young people have taken up arms against the Caliphate. The glimpsed horror is simply factored into the day-to-day course of things.[6]

INCAPABLE OF LOOKING AT "THAT"

It behooves us to know that the Caliphate's communications strategists are aware of our habits. They know that the Western public is incapable of looking at "that" and that the media will never show "it"[7] and that in fact everyone is recusing themselves from the ethical consequence of being a witness.

This moral deficit, analogous to that of the Polish peasant

who lived next to a German concentration camp but "saw nothing," is something the Caliphate is aware of: When we are denied by the mainstream media the opportunity to look at those videos and images, we are at the same time denied the moral responsibility that goes with becoming witnesses of the crimes they record. This is factored in by the Caliphate's communications strategists, who play with our self-righteous cowardice. Posting them online is therefore, for their part, a dare and a taunt, a rhetorical trap in which we fall headlong.

Lastly, it is unlikely that the public in the West would ever have easy access to either any television channel such as was announced[8] or to any radio broadcasts from regions where the Caliphate is active.[9] Unless such a channel were to adopt the same posture as the multitudinous Arab stations burgeoning in the Middle East or an international channel broadcasting in English. Which would be a different game altogether and would correspond to the consolidation of the Caliphate as a permanent state. It would mean that we had moved to a different, as yet undefined, model: a terrifying scenario of global television reach that is not altogether impossible.

In sum, confining ourselves to the video material: We must conclude that if the Caliphate employs these horrifying videos to frighten the West,[10] their impact is dubious. Either they are not seen, for reasons supposedly relating to media decency or censorship, or they are derided (black humor parodies of bleeding puppets on the Internet),[11] or they are the reserve of experts, or they are categorized as niche amateur pornography.[12] As to the "radicalization" effect, it remains to be proven that a video provokes such turmoil in a "young person" as to make him or her instantly convert and become a martyr.[13]

JIHADIST INTELLIGENCE

The documents prepared by the caliphal militants do not bear out this thesis, as previously noted. Also, reading the biographies of the young people who have chosen to join jihadism or the Caliphate, like the gifted high school student from Melbourne who fought to the death or the young Garland, Texas terrorist,[14] they do so after diligent research: They gather information, read, learn, and form opinions about the state of the world. They are not hooked on the so-called propaganda material. Others, along the lines of a Mehra, have most often followed religious fundamentalist courses or sermons that set them on the path of action.[15]

A habitual response, nonetheless, is that youth are "easily influenced."

To be sure, but then we need to explain how the Caliphate is a greater source of influence than, say, living in peace at home and joining, as some of those executed have, humanitarian aid groups. Or how these individuals, whether originally Muslim or not, are "made vulnerable" or have been "marginalized." But by what? In the case of those who have not yet converted: by the fact, precisely, that Western values are weak? And do not hold up against "strong" values? What exactly is a strong value? And how are our values weak? For Muslims, a puerile distinction is made between "good" and "bad" imams, as if qualifying imams solved the problem of the so-called superior attractiveness of "bad words."

Because, right away, the question arises of how the Muslim Brotherhood's[16] "strategy for action in the secular space" or the Islamic Organization for Education, Sciences, and Culture's "cultural strategy" is any different in its objectives from those, direct and lacking any circumlocution, of imams who point to the path of the Caliphate.[17]

Even if the Caliphate and the Muslim Brotherhood were not two irons in the fire of the same ambition, the question remains: Why would a westernized Islam have less of a hold on youth looking for ideals than the Caliphate's Islam? Except, of course, by saying that war, personal sacrifice, violence, and martyrdom are stronger? But to assert the primacy of violence is to wander into dangerous territory for those who wish to assert that humankind is essentially humble and peaceable. To argue that violent words carry more force, hence more practical value, than peaceful words is to argue that "man is (by nature) a wolf to man," as in the terse Roman saying revived by Thomas Hobbes in the seventeenth century, and that in politics "evil" is not accidental but essential. Conservative Christians may indeed, then, concur with the Caliphate's followers: Satan is the Prince of the World, violence is the rule of iron, and human politics is perverse in its essence. God's Rule must be brought forward. Whether this line of argument is sustainable in combating terrorism is, to say the least, self-defeating.

The upshot is simple: The goal of the videos and texts that

the Caliphate launches on the Internet is not to convert millions to armed struggle, to persuade massively. It does not fit the standard scenario of "mass persuasion."

So how does this material operate, if it is essentially created neither to terrify nor to market and peddle ideas?

We must look at the aesthetic side.

On Obedience

Jihadist propaganda is, nonetheless, distinct in spreading its influence in countries considered to be infidels by the Caliphate and carrying out its efforts in a language that is incomprehensible to many of its recruits. The young Canadian, the young man from Normandy, the young Australian, the young Kazakh (and even operatives from Trinidad and Tobago and Brazil) who respond to the call of the Caliphate—numbering in the thousands—rarely understand any Arabic, certainly not the classical tongue of Scriptures. What are they obeying?

LISTENING, OBEYING

Or rather, it is precisely Arabic that they hear. Better yet, that they see. They hear it and they see it without understanding it. They perceive, they feel, they take in sensation, which accurately describes an "aesthetic" attitude (from Ancient Greek *aisthēsis*, perception, sensation). An aesthetic judgment is judgment based on strong sensation experienced when seeing, for instance, a beautiful human being or an atrocious scene.

Better yet, to see, to hear, to obey, these three gestures summarize an even more calibrated definition of the "aesthetic."

In Ancient Greek philosophy, the source of the first Western political thought—and this is what we are concerned with, politics—lying together are a terrible word and the concept that gives it its power: *Aesthetic* comes from *aeô,* which means both "to hear" and . . . "to obey." *Audition* derives from this complex word and the notion it expresses. The great Greek playwrights employed it above all in choirs, which on stage represented the people, witnesses to terrifying events of the highest political order—involving gods, men, and the destiny of the world. All this was conveyed in representation through powerful images, extraordinary phraseology, engendering strong emotions and the involvement of the spectators.

The rhetorical montage of a high-stakes political drama turns on this extraordinary concept that engages us, beyond reason, in a domain of sensation that drives, elevates, and gives meaning. It forces adhesion or repulsion: to reject an atrocious video of the Caliphate's by blogging: "F—-s, kill 'em all!" (and there is much worse) is an aesthetic repulsion, an aesthetic judgment. It is obedience to image.

So, here we have a standard working model for understanding how, without knowing Arabic, the language of conversion, one can listen, see, obey. All at once.

There are two essential factors in jihadist aesthetics aimed at those who do not understand Arabic; this is as true of the videos, sometimes subtitled in English or French, as it is, naturally to a lesser degree, of the publications in these languages that contain beautiful arabesques, or translated, transliterated utterances, akin to an assemblage of storyboards and soundtracks. Example: "Are you *aslamtum?*": image (the picture or frame) + sound (the incomprehensible *aslamtum*, reduced to a sound-word or "scratch vocal") = to perceive a concept (the call to jihad). To perceive then = to obey ("islam" as submission by conversion). In sum, to be *aslamtum* is to submit to the power of this double perception by which a "sonic" idiom is rendered present by dint of images. Is this explanation far-fetched?

SENSORIAL CONVERSION

The process is in fact no different from conversions that, in the Middle Ages, were conducted in Latin, a language that no one outside of the clergy understood but that was, in a way, activated, illustrated, brought to life, in the aesthetics of the cathedral's stained glass, which recounted mystical tales through images that were simultaneously put into Latin, a language unknown to most, but of mystical sonic value. The holy storyboard perceived by the faithful on the stained glass and glossed over in the incomprehensible soundtrack of Latin sermons ensured, aesthetically, obedience. Knight crusaders who left home to liberate the Holy Sepulcher were just as illiterate. They had never read the Bible. Perceiving ideas takes many shapes, and that is a political lesson the Caliphate has inflicted upon us and that we do not seem to have fully understood, so subservient are we to rational thinking.

This comparison helps us understand why commentators who deride the lack of deep religious training by jihadist recruits overlook the crucial fact that one does not adopt an ideal, especially a religious one, after having read all the books available and conducted research—for most, a few words suffice: conversion is absolute, it is not relative to knowledge.[18] It is fundamentally aesthetic. It partakes of the sublime. Of course in the context of jihadist terror we recoil at that notion. But, again, facing up to reality is overdue, especially when, as we shall see in chapter 8, the Caliphate forces a confrontation.

Aesthetics possesses this hallucinatory power to transmit a message or to lay the ground for the reception of a message, even absent comprehension. We perceive it even when we do not conceive it.

On the picture side: In the inflationary abundance of visuals in circulation on the Internet, where everything is copied, pasted, banalized, reprised, rehashed, in short reduced to an exponential reproduction worn thin by repetition or to an imitation of the same (a "traffic" that exists simply to produce traffic, and hence revenue, for those furnishing it), the sounds and images of the Caliphate are jarring, they stupefy the targets of their persuasion that understand neither the arabesques nor the calligraphy. They provoke lingering over their images, stupefaction in the face of a thing new and exotic.

On the audio side: The chanting most often present on the soundtracks, before the speeches for example, accompanies texts or images. Even without understanding the words, it is impossible not to lend one's ear to them: The Arabic chanting is aesthetic, for if one extracts these fatidic chants from their context, their beauty is that of monastic chanting or, within the register of Islam, those of Nusrat Fateh Ali Khan, who has driven European audiences in London, Milan, and Paris to lyrical ecstasies.

Notably, the Caliphate specializes in the *nasheed*, choral chanting of undeniable lyricism: men's voices, modulated intoning. For example, the caliphal marching hymn:

And we sever heads by the strike of the sword,
And by striking the enemy we heal souls.
So take heed, my enemy, of the day of doom,
That old glory may arise in the world,
That old glory may arise in the world.[19]

Amid the chaos of rap and rock on the Internet, these caliphal choral works and these chants, at once religious and warlike, stand out. They compel. They underscore the absence of values of appeal that characterizes the everyday experience of materialism.

The diction of some radio announcements (for example, one that explains the Tunis attack in March 2015), the nobility of tone and phraseology jar with everything else on the Internet, the utter lack of formality that "citizen reporters" employ, addressing everyone as though they were a friend, whereas the jihadist announcers, to a greater or lesser extent, borrow the exacting techniques of Koranic recitation.[20]

Not understanding either the aesthetic of the calligraphy or the meaning of the texts and speeches does not result in rejection; on the contrary, it brings about adhesion—and that is the primary effect of obedience. The young Norwegian viewer, weary of his mediocre lower-middle-class "paradise," listens and watches and thinks: "Now, I must understand. I want to find out more."

The aesthetic prowess of the Caliphate lies in its having understood that to attract those who do not understand the language of conversion (Arabic), the sound and picture combination is an effective strategy. The persuasive strategy of strangeness and rupture is seductive: It is a window onto another universe that seems to be beyond repetition, beyond banality, beyond the daily grind. It re-enchants the world.[21] It gives it a new, enchanting meaning and inspires a transition from aesthetic attraction to ethical adherence, because to adhere to *jihad* is a moral choice, an awful one to be sure, but nonetheless a moral one.

How should we respond? By banalizing the phenomenon: circulating these publications in schools, subjecting them to textual commentaries and radical deconstructions, showing the videos and analyzing them with all our savoir-faire of film criticism, reducing these material documents to a pitiful state by means of rational proofs, as Western cultural tradition knows best: by thinking clearly, distinctly, and rationally, in particular about the irrational and the power of the senses.

SEVEN

Caliphal Feminism

During the first jihadist phase, the one gravitating around the axis of Al-Qaeda and sustained by Palestinian terrorism, women appeared on the scene as suicide bombers. This phenomenon caused consternation—in part because they were women, in part because of their youth—and sparked research on why they would choose this path.[1]

In the age of the Caliphate, there is a different discourse regarding women in the service of jihadism (other than as human bombs), and the interrogation is filtered, for it is not explicitly articulated (such is the game of ideology), through a European debate, particularly virulent in France and Belgium and increasingly so in Germany, on the question of the veil and the adventures of its interdiction.

There are numerous departures[2] and numerous conversions[3] and returns to the faith that are disconcerting.[4] In England,[5] the debate about women and Islam took a different turn as a result of the repeated scandals that culminated in the discovery of a system of forced prostitution of hundreds if not thousands of very young girls, tacitly allowed by an entire Muslim community and voluntarily passed over in silence by the social services, in the name of an ideology of non-intervention in community affairs (the press maintains the code of address by using "Asians" instead of "Muslims," since most are from Pakistan, hence Asia).[6] In the United States, women rarely join the Caliphate; when they do, their behavior quickly falls within the psychotherapeutic realm, or that of the mysterious temptress, until the facts emerge.[7]

In Germany, the media's angle of attack is that of the dominant discourse,[8] the precautionary path of the *multikulti*. However, as it is in France that the number of women jihadists is the greatest, in the hundreds, let us turn our attention there.[9]

Feminist Codes

In France, this sociological fact is obscured by the French use of a rhetorical code that relegates women to a specific category in public debate, *"le statut de la femme"* (women's status), both explicitly (by the press and political professionals, for example) and implicitly (in everyday life) in schools, in offices, and in social exchanges.

This code is the outcome of combining two feminisms. It is a tributary of French feminism which was and remains both philosophical, literary, and libertarian in its origins: a militant feminism, often anti-male and strikingly intolerant of religion. This feminism hails from the revolutionary feminism of 1789, obliterated by Napoleonic machismo until the slow reforms of the education of "girls" in the middle of the nineteenth century, arriving at its climax with the 1975 legalization of abortion by a liberal-conservative government. Twenty years ago, this philosophical militant feminism, which ought to have seen Simone de Beauvoir receive a Nobel Prize, encountered a different feminism, which came from the Anglo-American world: "gender theory."

From the French standpoint this style of feminism is, for all intents and purposes, a branch of the social sciences and especially behaviorism: It postulates that sexual identity is the result of a "social construct" wherein the biological is a basis, and only a basis. Sexual identity, "gender," is piled atop this foundation like a social and behavioral Lego set and is called "cultural" (in the Anglo-Saxon anthropological sense, not in the French civilizational sense).

For a long time, these ideas were in France the preserve of an intellectual elite. But when they finally entered public debate, by a natural process of vulgarization they were rephrased in the now-common language of social interaction: that of management. The "woman" question became that of a human resource to be managed in the most optimal way. The invasion of entire sections of public discourse by management language allowed the consolidation of a fixed code of what had previously been a specialized rhetoric with regard to "women" as a social subject.

As a result of this construct, it was intellectually possible in French public discourse to manage the tension between the rhetorical code regarding "women" (political "parity," sexual liberation, the right to their own bodies, workplace equal treatment) and the Palestinian women carrying bombs by implicitly arguing, through a process of rationalization, that these women were the objects of male power of which the veil was a soft symbol and that it was therefore the equivalent of the explosives belt; the one was inside a deliberative political culture, the other inside a masculine culture of violence and of war; consequently, it was possible to be feminist and to want the interdiction of the veil.

But with the Caliphate, another language, a radical one, on women appears. It destabilizes five codes of discourse that had hitherto framed the question, in France but also in Italy and Spain and, to a lesser degree, Germany: the prevalent, feminist opinion on "women"; the intellectual debate on gender; the attempts at the adoption of these two codes in the Francophone Maghreb;[10] the old code of the woman Palestinian kamikaze; and the idea of an Arabo-Muslim "post-ideological"[11] feminism.

Another feminist discourse has taken shape before our eyes: caliphal feminism, which stunned the French media before becoming a transnational concern. The Caliphate has been a game-changer in terms of challenging the Western notion of feminism.

What does the Caliphate say on the subject of women? There

is a manifesto from January 2015 on the status of women according to and within the Caliphate.[12] In *Dābiq*[13] it was followed by a confession, or profession, of faith by a female emigrant (this is the translation of the Arab term designating a woman that chooses to depart for the Caliphate). The open letter describes departure from a country where immorality reigns to a country where one can live in accordance with one's principles, a militant pilgrimage of no return toward the land of true Islam.

The Female Emigrant, the Female Face of Jihad

The account by this female emigrant is of a return to God, in the theological sense of the word *conversion* (*convertere* in Latin, "to revert"), a return to God and a reconciliation with the people of God that is also a gesture of repentance for having remained apart from it and from them.[14] All religions and all powerful ideologies stimulate or impose a return by the individual to the principle and place that animates them and gives them their *raison d'être*, through pilgrimages, processions, or marches—all are devotional terms and practices that designate movement toward a source. These themes are explicit both in this narrative and in the rest of the testimonials by female emigrants.

This account, several pages long in perfect English, echoes the remarks of hundreds of educated and determined women who have undertaken this journey of return. The text is a montage that, based on their experiences of leaving the land of the infidel and returning to the country of God, extracts codes and narratives in order to systematize them. The production delivers in condensed form the essentials of accounts and rhetorical codes of the emigrant female such as it is and such as the Caliphate wishes it to be.

The emigrant female is repeating the gesture, the "tribulation," of Muhammad leaving Mecca for Yathrib/Medina, in other words leaving the city of apostates and idolaters to rejoin the community of believers. What we have is a true pilgrimage toward the lands of Islam.[15] Or, to cite the widow of Coulibaly, alias Abou Bassir Abdallah al Ifriqi, after her arrival in the Caliphate:

> Praise be to Allah who made my journey possible. I had no difficulty getting here. . . . It is a good thing to live on land that is ruled by the laws of Allah. I am relieved to have fulfilled this obligation."[16]

This departure and return are also a rejection of tribal organization and an affirmation of the universality of Mohammedanism ("beyond languages and the color of the skin, our hearts are one with the unique God"). Such is the code of the return: to join that community of believers, not a territory governed by this or that bloodline, genealogy, or affiliation, but a place where the universality of faith is affirmed.

So the letter explains that contrary to what Western propaganda states, the "sisters" who emigrate and undertake their *hegira* are "not marginalized by poverty, unemployment, familial or psychological problems" (the usual categories enlisted to explain "radicalization"). Their true marginalization is caused by living in immorality, outside the land of believers.

In a nutshell, the West is the margin, the essential marginalization. Contrary to the "cultural strategy" of implantation advocated by Muslim organizations in Europe and America[17]—practical, tactical, tacit, or public recipes for putting up with life in places where infidels decide on a Muslim's way of life—this is not about putting up but about leaving. There is no other stratagem for women, other than to leave.

The second rhetorical code is that of the autonomy of the emigrant woman relative to the family group.

The woman that decides to return, modeling herself on the earliest emigrant women who undertook their *hegira* at the time of the foundation of Mohammedanism, is defying or shattering her family ties; there is no need for the consent or the accompaniment of her husband, her father, or her brother—or any male relative:

> This is a secondary debate . . . a sister that emigrates transcends familial obstacles to take part in a long and difficult journey on which god will watch over her, a journey filled with emotion, and in time, with memories.

The *hegira* by the emigrant is an act of autonomy and of individual responsibility, a feminist act, in flagrant contrast to the "cultural strategy" of an Islam implanted in Europe that privileges men:

> The question of the condition of women cannot be addressed as such but must be re-situated within a broader framework . . . [namely] that the most important question is that of man's liberation from an archaic stagnation where habits take precedence over religion.[18]

This feminism of emigrating women is on a collision course with the West's feminism on the chapter on children:[19] Whereas a common theme of Western feminism today is the right to an abortion, to lose a child in the name of the rights of the female body, the feminist on a *hegira* also asserts her right to lose her child, but in another way.

Not in the name of her body but in the name of the spiritual body of the community of believers. The feminist on a *hegira* asserts the right to depart when pregnant even if, due to the strains of the journey, the child is at risk of dying, for it will be buried in the land of Islam, in the land where its "primordial human nature," or *fitra*, is known and understood, a far better outcome for that child than to be spiritually dead amid the teachings of the idolatrous. This is what the text spells out.

So, the rights over one's body are connected to something else, through feminism: to departing from a culture, the Western one, that wreaks spiritual, hence physical ruin, as "primordial human nature" is "integrative." Whereas abortion does not address the question of this integrative quality (all that counts is the body of the woman having the abortion), the risk of losing the child due to a tribulation, which is a form of infanticide for its part, addresses the integrality of human nature: A still-born infant is reborn by being interred in the land of Islam. It is restored "integrally" to the community.

The third code is the exaltation of the moment of the return and the militant re-disposition that emanates from this return:

> And even were I to forget everything, I never will forget the moment our feet touched the good earth of Islam and the moment we saw the black banner of the Prophet waving in the wind before us . . . our lips murmured "God is great . . ." it was for this that these women had left behind them country, family, friends, to be able to live under the purview of the holy law.

The key term that emerges, however, is *slave*. The emigrant women declare themselves to be "slaves of God." The expression means that by assuming such a position—the result of a deliberate act, the individual *hegira*—these women now in the holy lands have accomplished an exact return, a conversion completed. Which gives them the right to admonish "these half-men" who want to block the emigrating women:[20]

> And to those who, under the pretext of good counsel, rise to prevent you from leaving, I say: your women are better men than you!

Here is a feminist practice, a gender code, that is a far cry from the maneuvers inherent to the cultural strategy of the Muslim

Brotherhood on wearing or not wearing a veil, which depends on how a given localized Western community may reject or tolerate Muslim ostentatiousness. As the emigrant women say, that is "a secondary problem," for all accommodation is secondary. Women have been also in combat—celebrated as the modern successors of historical Muslim women of exemplary courage and virtue.

Here we find a principled position that the feminist rhetoric, described earlier, is reluctant to consider and to countenance. Faced with this feminism out of the ordinary, Western feminism has become peripheral, disarmed, aphonic. Who, among Western feminists, can respond to the jihadist poet Ahlam al-Nasr, whose lyricism engenders such unprecedented fervor among women marching toward the Caliphate or marching to battle under the banner of ISIS?[21] As of yet the gauntlet has not been picked up, rhetorically or otherwise.

EIGHT

Warrior Virility

Jihadist soldiers appear on our screens, strapped for action and lashing with words. Male eloquence in battle dress. A virile *mise en scène* of the warrior. Confronting us. In our face.

But what is its rhetoric? How has it been constructed? From the jihadist soldier's appearance to his interface with us, the enemy?

Ethics of Ostentation

Black and sand are the colors of the uniforms of the soldiers of God—without fourragères, without epaulettes, without badges, without stripes, without signs of hierarchy or valor. Battle dress brought down to its barest abstraction to display the warrior body. And this apparition leads to the recognition of virile strength.

Black. The black uniform of the Caliphate's military is a sartorial triumph, troubling in its beauty. This obsidian warrior bodice, espousing and molding war-hardened forms—not muscles artificially produced by visits to a gym—whether it appears in beheading videos or in online propaganda films, is a *mise en scène* of virile seduction. Borrowed from specialized uniforms and the body armor of special forces, the jihadist black combat gear confirms that, even without the full protection of Seyntex or Kevlar, the Caliphate's soldiers advance, at once vulnerable and terrifying. This is a metaphor.

Sand. The desert camouflage uniform and hood are an apparel response to the combat uniforms of Western forces in the Levant.[1] Not a carbon copy reply but a theatrical reply: The Caliphate is affirming the visual codes of reference, organizational and military, of caliphal forces. Its reply to the enemy is: We are the desert, not you. This too is a metaphor.

Masked faces. The black uniform that sheathes the warrior body to display its dangerousness to better effect, the hood that reduces the face to a piercing gaze the cameramen of the Caliphate zoom in on, these are acts of defiance and of seduction. The hood is the analogue, on the masculine side, to the veil on the feminine side. The uniform of the militants dissimulates, the better to fascinate. It is a game of masks.

Bare faces. The militants often appear with their faces uncovered: The half-brother of Mohammed Mehra, in a video that shows him haranguing an adolescent in French and ordering him to execute an Arab suspected of being a Mossad agent, does so with his face uncovered.[2] In another video, a child with long hair, a Kazakh, executes two Russian prisoners.[3] The assassin of a British soldier, in 2013, operates with his face bare and makes sure he is being filmed. There are numerous examples, among them Maxime Hauchard.[4]

Uncovered. The foreign soldiers of the Caliphate,[5] because they symbolize and materialize conversion or a return to faith and the assembling of God's people, show themselves, recount their journeys, and narrate their battles. Even partisans barely bother erasing their trail: Against the rules of a secret war, they advance, their faces virtually uncovered. If intelligence agencies identify them rapidly after the engagement, it is precisely because they are offering themselves up as "open sources."[6] The official videos and various magazines show the faces of the militants and name them when they fall on the field of honor. The Caliphate's polyglot periodicals have galleries of martial martyrs. The Caliphate's jihadist is seen and must be seen.

This codified montage of warrior virility may be qualified as "theatrical";[7] it is, in fact, an ethical montage, for there are neither sets, nor actors, nor fake victims. We are confronted with an ethics of virility in action.

The Warrior's Radiance

In fact, this desire for recognition is a strategy for affirming an unwavering presence: to be physically recognized and to receive the ethical gratitude of those who follow the Caliphate, of the Caliph himself. Thus the celebration of the "lions,"[8] the heroes of the Caliphate who form a sort of military nobility by their sacrifice of themselves: This system of recognition is structural, it is ostentatious in its severity.

If a war is believed to be just, then it must be ostentatious: This is something we no longer wish to admit in an age where wars are conducted in secret or without risk and avoid (the Iraq invasion notwithstanding) the spectacular, what might be called the display of a just power that is superior to, and greater than, simple power. Tragically and perversely we care to display ostentatious martial radiance when coffins of fallen soldiers are unloaded, draped, and honored. We are ostentatious in mourning alone.

Western regimes have effectively become symbolically impotent: Their capital in ostentation has been squandered, and their ability to comprehend the ethical power of ostentation has atrophied. They no longer express the force of "being here" that imposes respect—a block to the enemy, the long gaze (*respectum*, in Latin) in the face of power, whose capacity to turn into material force is recognizable and can, in turn, be transmitted at will.

The Caliphate, however, forces us to engage in a martial confrontation: a face to face.

On Warring

Suddenly, we are face to face. The Caliphate's Islamic State Hacking Division posts names, addresses, and photographs of a hundred or so American military men and women. The American services have confirmed at least two other pirating incidents, but they succeeded in stopping the propagation of those ID photographs in time.[9]

This is a direct response by the Caliphate to the regular publication of the names of "designated terrorists" by the U.S. State Department.[10] But while these lists are like abstract, bureaucratic files, the pirating of accounts reveals the identity of the families of the military enemy that it designates for violent action: "Knife them as they walk in the street and believe they are safe."[11]

The message is one of limitless war, a war with no zone of protection or refuge: a war where nobody is safe from the face to face.

Thus the Caliphate personalizes war.

Asymmetric War and Virtuous War

To Western aerial or robotized long-distance violence or to furtive special ops, the Caliphate responds with violence that is personal and face to face. It responds to the anonymity of aerial strikes with personal attacks. The conduct of war by Western allies, which has become a long-distance action tending toward impersonality, is reestablished at the level of waging war in a direct and personal way.

An explanation: Since the Korean War and its aftermath—the balance of nuclear terror—Western democracies have favored "asymmetric war." Democracies fight wars but do not like waging wars that carry a human cost on their side. They seek technological asymmetry to vanquish their enemies.

Hence, democracies employ their technological advantages to avoid contact and to minimize risks, in particular by air strikes[12] ("strike warfare") assisted by robotization.[13] Whence the habitual recourse to air strikes since the first Gulf War (1990), then the pillorying of Serbia, Iraq, Afghanistan, and now Syria.

Strategists at times connect the notion of asymmetric war[14] with a second notion, that of a "virtuous war":

> The technical capacity and ethical necessity (when a state
> for example "mistreats its people" or that the UN mandates
> an intervention) to threaten and to actualize long-distance
> violence—while minimizing losses (for the attacking side).[15]

Virtue, here, has little to do with ethics but resides in the reality of minimizing the loss of materials and men and unnecessary expense.

Military drones are thus the natural prolongation of the so-called "risk aversion" process, a term that comes from the financial risk management sector. Virtuous war is, therefore, the result of an asymmetry that allows the legal and massive use of force framed by the management of war ("minimizing costs") that has prevailed over combat.[16] This is the rhetorical construction of a self-absorbed management language by strategists and for state organizations, language that the Caliphate explodes with a return to warring virility and the cult of contact.

Our concept of war, therefore, is hygienic: long-distance weapons, as few victims on our side as possible, as many on the other side as possible—not sparing, in Iraq nor in Afghanistan, for example, when the parameters of the strike are inaccurate, village wedding ceremonies or hospitals. The number of civilian victims is terrifying, but it is not a number that concerns us, as it takes place, once again, "at a distance," whereas it is a personal reality on the ground for the victims.[17]

For with this management rhetoric of a long-distance war, it is we who anesthetize ourselves in the face of the violence that is perpetrated. It is significant that we subscribe to a line of reasoning that is indistinguishable from cliché: When a police officer is killed during an attack, he is a "hero fallen in the line of duty." For the Caliphate, a soldier who dies in action is a martyr, that is, a "heroic witness." Our depictions of fallen police officers or soldiers often refer to their families and communities, but this personalization in effect makes their actions less warlike, and dead operatives less actual killing agents and more ordinary people. We personalize the warring dead only to make them less lethal.

By contrast, the Caliphate reestablishes a true personalization of war, changes the notion of risk, muddies the map of moral superiority (since its appeal too, to its soldiers and partisans, is ethical), and forces us to look war in the face.

The Caliphate returns to war its virility, that is to say it restores a "warrior virtue" that has nothing to do with the management concept of a war with no risk. It restores true proximity to it. The Caliphate takes the personalization of war to its logical end.

The Caliphate is therefore taking us back to the metaphysical sources of war: *Bellum,* "war," is an extension of *duellum,* "the duel," an event that takes place in direct contact, mediated only by a weapon, in a face to face. It is time, perhaps, for warfare as duel to replace our impersonal risk management of war. Or at least to realize that the war waged on democracies by jihadism is a resilient and unwavering search for a violent, personal face to face: After all, is not a terror attack a ghastly act of proximity? The sooner we adapt our vocabulary and arguments, the better equipped we will be to face up to this new reality, with or without the Caliphate.

This virility of close combat then takes on a second, stupefying form: that of human sacrifice.

NINE

Islamic Porno-Politics

He brandishes a knife in a studied gesture, and having memorized his text or using a teleprompter he threatens the West, France, America, and, according to what is now an established ritual, slits someone's throat. Of course, other than by navigating the Internet, which would then expose you to ongoing police surveillance for visiting sites blocked or watched by intelligence agencies, few of us have been able or willing to see the bloody scene in its entirety. Televisions show only a blurred detail, made emblematic by the orange overalls, themselves modeled on the garb that political prisoners in Guantánamo were once made to wear.

The media, prudishly, never show the execution. Still, what is shown, even reduced to images that imply and permit the notion of the execution, is a surprising act.

The terrorist, the one who, in the scene staged by the Caliphate, slits throats, marks the reappearance of an extraordinary dimension of politics that, since the Jewish genocide and to a lesser degree Hiroshima, and with distasteful discretion in the case of the Gulag, had been enshrined in codes of blame. These codes refer to the politics of an era during which politics was indeed unmanageable, a political time and space marked by the imperious presence of "evil."

Owing to these codes of blame the West had succeeded, since 1945, not in expelling violence from politics but in acclimatizing it. And when put face to face with forms of evil in politics (the irresistible follow-up to the local wars since 1945 and African massacres on a grand scale), we have been capable of managing its effects and its images, in short, of reducing its effects, to the point of often absolving its actors. This is what the oft-repeated expression "the banality of evil" means: In the end, we made political evil (not "evil itself") banal, manageable, integratable.

With beheadings in broad daylight, in quasi–real time, a different phenomenon has come about: the rise of a form of unmanageable political evil. We repeated "never again this," but the "this" that has arisen now is a different "this," a violence flaunted, glorified, aestheticized, endorsed by an (ethical, in the Caliphate's view) exigency, but one that is also Ubu-esque, vile, grotesque, inhuman—porno-politics.[1]

What to Call "This"?

To manage porno-politics, the unthinkable "this," we need, at the very least, to name it, so we resort to familiar codes ("executioner, torturer, savage, barbarian"), and bloggers spill trashy expletives all over the Web by the cartload, all of which are naive and instinctive attempts to manage the face to face with evil using language. Often the act of naming at random relieves one from thinking.

But our glossary for expressing evil suffers from depreciation: How can we say the Caliphate's beheader is a "barbarian" when we say that kicking a cat is an act of barbarism? Or how can we call him a "savage" when hoodlums who terrorize French suburban trains are also characterized as savages?

"Beheading"? For a long while the media did not know whether throat-slittings should be called beheadings instead. "Beheading" prevailed in English, French, German, and other European languages to qualify what is intentionally (and even judicially) a throat-slitting, followed indeed by a severing of the head and, sometimes, a crucifixion of the headless body. In France that hesitation was compounded by national history: *décapitation,* or beheading, belongs to a manageable political code dating back to the fall of the monarchy. Enemies of the Revolution, royals, aristocrats, and above all priests were beheaded. In effect, saying in French *décapitation* to specify the slitting of the throats of the Caliphate's victims amounts to saying that the Islamic henchmen are on the side of justice, in the same manner that the French revolutionaries were, while those who were "decapitated" were on the side of evil. This is of course particular to France, but it provides a vivid or sordid illustration of the perils of not naming an act for what it is, in this case throat-slitting.

The state of confusion in naming the scenes of throat-slitting is such that we have reached the point of saying the opposite of what codes would require us to do to keep evil outside of politics.

Again, since France has been at the front line of Islamic attacks by commandos or partisans of the Caliphate, it is worth noting that recent French political history has known henchmen: The German occupiers were labeled, still are labeled, "henchmen" (*les bourreaux*—although the periphrastic epithet "Nazi" has replaced "German" in view of the two nations' reconciliation). At the time, the German occupier was transformed from an enemy into a henchman. In confusion, a term that had been reserved only for an officer of justice, charged with solemnly executing a death penalty, was then applied to the occupier, as if France were being punished by History at the malevolent hands of a malefic power beyond what humanity would be capable of "in normal circumstances."

Therefore, one might have thought "henchman" would become the generic term with which to qualify jihadist terrorists. The term has not caught on. Why? Especially considering that in the case of the German occupiers and of the concentration camp workers the term was used and continues to be used? What is stopping us? What distinguishes the German henchman that used to hang prisoners by their thumbs using thin steel wires while tying heavy stones to their other limbs until they died of atrocious suffering, while murmuring "Vive la France," from the terrorist that executes a Christian, kneeling in front of him and crying out: "Jesus! Jesus!" before having his throat slit?

That the Caliphate is not occupying France is not a good reason: The multiple terrorist acts by the partisans of jihadism on the national soil should suffice to point out that occupation is part of the package (see chapter 8).

No. If we refrain from saying "henchman," it is because, faced with the scene of beheading by a soldier or partisan of the Caliphate, we confusedly experience the simultaneity both of evil, as a dimension integral to politics, and of sacrifice, as an operator of political evil.

We thought we had purged politics of evil and of sacrifice. They have returned, and this return is irreversible. The terrorist facing us is performing a sacrifice. Of the psychological operations the Caliphate might be said to mount,[2] this is the most radical: the resurrecting of the performer of sacrifices.

Sacrificial Rites of Porno-Politics

The beheadings are staged to represent the sacred as we had forgotten it, but as it remains deeply etched in the mind. They belong to politics as a form of pornography, and it is no coincidence that videos of beheadings first found an avid public on Internet sites peddling gore.

The sacred, when it takes the stage, must be "phenomenal."[3] The beheading scenes are phenomenal realities in the sense that they demonstrate a phenomenon that is real but also extraordinary, "phenomenal": the sacrificatory dimension of politics at the dawn of the twenty-first century. Secular or materialist societies deprived of the sense of the sacred, especially countries like Germany and France that are, by and large, de-Christianized have nonetheless retained an atavistic sense of the phenomenal power of sacrifice, seen bursting forth on the screens in reality scenes of actual sacrifice.[4]

Anthropology of the Throat-Slitting Soldier

The ritual of terrorist beheadings is a liturgy in which a soldier performs a religious act. By contrast, an officer who commands an execution platoon is executing an order. Nothing religious even in the *coup de grâce*. The terrorist making a sacrifice, for his part, is not a member of the military executing an order but an acolyte adopting the twin mantles of religious and military power, which explains the anthropological intersection that produces the sacrifice.

A part of the fear we feel when faced with these repeated and spectacular acts stems from the fact that they are at once military and liturgical. The outrageousness of such a military-religious fusion is clear. Our anthropological references (as we think about the human, a logic of *anthropos*) fail us, for we are in the presence of another anthropological reality.

Let us compare this with Iranian Islam: Despite wars and battles, internal and external, since the dethroning of the Shah and the Shi'ite awakening, have we ever seen a soldier of the Iranian Islamic revolution harangue the world and behead anyone?[5] No, because this is not his function.

In fact, Iranians and Europeans together make up a single anthropological zone, Indo-European culture, wherein the functions of society are divided into three distinct agencies. First, the religious and political function that has led to the development of state bureaucracies based on models of Church administration, the transfer of electoral modes of monastic origin to secular assemblies, and, of course, the transfers of the inducements offered by religious power into secular democratic structures.[6] Second, the military and police functions, which are regulated by law. Third, the productive function of goods and economic values.

In Iran, which is an Indo-European culture, the clergy lead, the Guardians of the Revolution protect, the people work—it is the model described by Plato in *The Republic*, a tri-functional model.[7]

Our Western anthropology of the political and social world therefore hinges on the identification of this triple distinction among those who administer sovereign power in the name of values commonly conceded to be superior (the Republic, the Nation); those who protect the community in the name of the law and through the legitimate and regulated exercise of force; and those who create and maintain communal wealth through work and commerce. Each function has its place, and through a structure of integration, each is equal in strength to the other. The triple functionality is recognizable in the democratic organization of the executive branch (state and administration), the judiciary (the law and the defense of the law) and the legislative (representing the nation as a source of wealth).

With the geographical exception of Iran, the anthropological zone within which the Semitic and Arabo-Muslim world falls, however, does not recognize this triple distribution of functions. And this has a direct bearing on sacrifice.

An Arabo-Islamic soldier can act as the performer of a religious sacrifice and articulate his act as such, in the course of the liturgy of a human sacrifice. He is accumulating two functions, the first and the second. Or rather, he does not accumulate them, as they do not exist in that distinct state in his anthropological mindset. He is rather responding to the Semitic notion of a "chosen people" of God, a status he arrogates as a criterion for action, an "election" that is forever and violently enacted at the expense of those who do not profess it or who care nothing about it, or to whom it is denied. It is an anthropological belief common to Semites, Arab-Muslims, and religious Jews alike. No Indo-European culture has ever believed that a deity had singled out among themselves a specific nation as the chosen one.

In the midst of our postmodernity, the Muslim soldier performing a sacrifice, in brutal and visible fashion, has resurfaced, bringing with him an ancient anthropological belief system; politics as pornography, a resilient cultural instinct—the powerful "residues" of pre-logical[8] thought rooted in a decisive anthropological substratum.

Military beheading, then, adopts all the codes of a liturgy.

Sacrificial Liturgy

As with any ritual, everything here is codified: the timeframe, the spatial frame, the storyboard frames. The principle of ritual is that it is recognizable and repetitive. A ritual that changes its images, gestures, and sequence is no longer a ritual, it is an event. Our mistake is to turn each beheading into an event instead of observing the framework of ritual. Here, again, we are snared by our mediatized attachment to event-centric narratives, to "breaking news."

The religious-military sacrifice, therefore, like any liturgy, has a calendar: The Caliphate announces that there is going to be a sacrifice; then follows the anguished wait, and the film of the sacrifice erupts; then come the commentaries by the Caliphate in its periodicals and messages; and the replay: announcement, wait, sacrifice, commentary; repeat. In order to be imposing, a liturgy must be a ritual, and a ritual must be repetitive.[9]

The ritual, aside from this temporal framework, is inscribed within a highly symbolic spatial framework: ground that is red or yellow or the color of sand (whether a desert or a riverbank or even a stage set), a sky or sea of a dazzling blue, and human statues, some in orange (the kneeling victims), others in black (performer of the sacrifice, standing), or the two hieratic friezes with the performers of sacrifice behind those being sacrificed.

All ritual acts require norms (the plans) and repetitions (the gestures).

Internet pundits who make fun of the paucity of material employed by the Caliphate for these scenes of sacrifice are missing the point: This is not cinema, it is reality, it is religious reality that demands the permanence of such codes, for only the permanence of the codes allows the imposing weight of the sacred to be felt. Religion demands repetition.

Execution videos follow a storyboard that is strictly codified, frame by frame, and "scratch vocal" by scratch vocal: The victim pronounces a speech of confession or of expiation, the performer of the sacrifice a moralizing speech of accusation, wherein the one being sacrificed serves as an example from which general admonitions are drawn. Additionally, one cannot eliminate the hypothesis according to which some of the earliest victims (humanitarian aid workers or human rights militants) shared the point of view of their assassins, since they themselves had gone onto the field to make reparations for the evils perpetrated by their own governments,[10] as they put it on occasion. Their last words, in these cases, were in effect speeches of expiation.

Both speeches, one expiatory, the other exhorting, follow another immutable code and ritual of sacrifice: Victims expiate, by way of words, what they have done in actions, and what they say is used as a model. In the most recent videos, the execution is preceded by a long interview, far from the scene of the sacrifice, in the course of which the victim undergoes a self-critique.

The ritual was short-circuited once only, by a counter-sacred disruption: In the course of the sacrifice of twenty Coptic Christians, the murderers, unable to hope that these "Nazarenes" should pronounce apostasy and convert to Islam *in extremis*, could not prevent those being sacrificed from crying out: "Jesus! Jesus!"[11] But a Christian ready to submit to martyrdom recognizes evil when he sees it. A Westerner, deprived of any religious culture, has no bearings other than words devoid of any meaning ("barbarians," "savages,") traversed by a pornographic shudder of horror.

As for the one performing the sacrifice, his harangue is a moral exhortation that can be judged revolting but that must, rhetorically, be taken for what it is: an obligation. In order for the sacrifice to appear as an act of justice, the enemy needs to be told its reason; on the other hand, the exhortation is addressed to those still searching for the righteous path, that of the Caliphate.

In fact, the individual sacrificed provides an occasion for which the performer of the sacrifice outlines, by analogy, a general schema that concerns us: The victim is not beheaded "to serve as an example," for ritual is not an act of reprisal (in a war of occupation you kill to set an example, so that people keep to the straight and narrow, so that they don't repeat the example of an uprising). Here, the sacrifice is a politico-religious obligation.

It is the combination of the discourse of expiation and the discourse of exhortation that propels the message and, in the mediatized Arabo-Muslim world (as opposed to the world of Western media), endows it with unrivaled power. The scene of the sacrifice is a scene of moral propaganda. It is useless to cover our face: Expiation and sacrifice are acts of morality.

But, at the risk of stating the obvious, what is being sacrificed is a human body.

From Insult to Mutilation

Sacrifice is a return of the body into politics. How and why?

Manipulating the human body is a constant of politics:[12] from the pre-nineteenth-century use of torture to the mistreatment of prisoners and the mentally ill in the nineteenth century, from the mutilating techniques of boys' hygiene to the restraining of women "hysterics," the body has passed into politics through successive phases of manipulation. For the last forty-odd years the human body as political object, in the West, has been articulated in precise legal objects, namely abortion, preventative medicine, and the right to die, all three of which are instances of legally sparing the body a perceived ill: preventing it from having to give birth, preventing it from having to be sick, preventing it from being forced to die badly. The body has been entirely secularized and placed under medical management techniques.

With the sacrifices perpetrated by the Caliphate, however, the human body as political object is brought back front and center suddenly—both the body of the performer of sacrifice (see the preceding chapter) and the body of the sacrificed. The body is a part of the picture, and it is evidently intolerable, so intolerable that we must not have access to these atrocious videos. The Caliphate reminds us that the body is a political object.

What happens to the bodies that are sacrificed? No one ever addresses this question. Do they have graves "worthy of their dignity"? Do these cadavers have a stone over them so that they might one day become tombs, places of reflection for those of the same religion, the same country? No. They are probably left to rot.

The sacrifice, therefore, begins with invective and ends with a profanation of the body: In keeping with practices of armed Algerian Islamic groups, the materiality of violence on the body of the enemy follows a precise rhetoric that proceeds from injury to insult to humiliation, then to death and mutilation and, finally, to the profanation of the cadaver.[13] This gradual process is a symbolic system of canceling the enemy body: The enemy no longer exists, not even as a cadaver.

Indeed, the Caliphate has rendered the process of sacrifice systematic, and hence strategic, by making it serial: Each execution has exemplary value in a determined category (each execution falls into a category: a journalist, a humanitarian aid worker, Christians, apostates, traitors, spies); each execution is reprised for apologetic purposes in glossy publications (an execution carries with it a teaching on this or that aspect of the struggle); each execution allows for the valorization of a soldier's or partisan's own martyrdom as an example to follow.

So there is more to sacrificial terrorism: the transformation of the enemy into nothing and of the soldier of the Caliphate into everything.

Those sacrificed do not become saints or heroes. They do not become anything: They become nothing. The terrorist performing the sacrifice tells us this, to our face and face to face: You are denied. You are nothing.

The reply to this denial of our existence is not to be found in the preventive management of terrorism—for to prevent is already to admit that evil exists powerfully—but in a public, and political, interrogation of this irreversible crossing of an anthropological red line, where, slowly, we are forced into no longer recognizing the salutary distinctions dividing the order of politics, the order of power, and the order of wealth. Self-pity is not a political virtue.[14]

We must resist this vision of a world where only "the chosen," in the religious sense of the word, count, and where everything else is sacrificed. The riposte is to be found in our own ethical fount.[15] So, as a next step, we must explain why Westerners change, body and soul, by joining the Caliphate and effectively convert twice: first from Western secularism to faith, and then from faith to Islam.

TEN

Inexplicable Terrorist?

How do we explain a French citizen, born and bred, becoming a soldier of the Caliphate? This same question was asked in America some time ago, as well as in Germany: How can an American or German turn into something inexplicable?

America, 1953:[1] After the Korean Armistice, twenty thousand prisoners were parked in neutral territory in a camp where each of the warring countries (North and South Korea, China, the United States) went to retrieve their own.

Problem: Many did not wish to be repatriated. Each side, therefore, sent groups to "explain" to their own nationals why it was better to come back home. This mission, overseen by the UN, was known as the United Nations Command Repatriation Group (UNCRG), and its mission was to give explanations to soldiers resisting repatriation. Still, all of them (Chinese, both kinds of Korean, Americans) had a choice: here or there?

The affair took on the proportions of a national crisis in the United States, because twenty or so young soldiers refused to come back home. Officials tried everything to explain to them why they should return, they vaunted the merits of the country. No way. So then they had to explain to the families, to people, to the nation, why "our boys" were refusing to comply. A press campaign. A scandal. The "boys" never gave in; they stayed where they wanted to be, and they did not return.

Medical explanation for the American public: The "boys" had been "brainwashed." The expression became current due to this event: Our "boys" chose to stay over there with the Reds! They must have been brainwashed.

The "boys," exasperated at not being treated as adults who had suffered war and prison, at being reduced to indoctrinated children, renamed themselves "the Unexplained," those who do not have to be told why they chose to stay on the side of the enemy. The last time the UNCRG came to visit, they unfurled a banner, "We are the Unexplained."

The young men that convert and join the brigades of the Caliphate are "unexplained" ("losers," as a French minister[2] scornfully called them, in English): Have they been brainwashed, all the way to the radix of their cortex, "radicalized"?

West Germany, 1976: Surgeons opened up the cranium of Ulrike Meinhof, the amazon terrorist of the RAF (Red Army

Faction). They passed along the criminal evidence to neurologists, who dissected the brain of the extremist muse in search of the causes of her terrorist tendencies. It was essential to explain in medical terms what appeared to be a mental aberration: being a terrorist, in West Germany, in 1970. Impossible that Ulrike should have chosen her terrorist engagement, albeit in the grand revolutionary tradition of the nineteenth century. She had to be diagnosed a mental patient. She could no more have chosen the Red Terror than the "boys" could have chosen Chinese communism.

In this scene of dissection, it was no longer a matter of accusing presumed chemical or physiological methods of "washing" the brain; instead terrorist zones had to be detected in the brain matter itself. The explanation was radically medicalized. It led to nothing. Had it led to something, would we lobotomize all "at-risk"[3] youth going forward? That would have to be the last word in the control over the body evoked earlier.

Today, nobody is suggesting that we dissect the brains of jihadists. In 1976, the idea would have been floated. Too bad, some would say. 1976 is not very long ago.

What remains of these phantasmagoria in white lab coats is an explanatory rhetoric: the medicalizing explanation. In the United States, the thesis of autism has been advanced to explain a conversion to jihadism, whereas a read of the young man's messages demonstrates fine mental maturity[4] (unless we extend psychological incrimination to all beliefs that fall outside commonly held opinions). So, we have medicalized and invented, in order to "explain," a medicalizing rhetoric at the service of politics; because to say that we have discovered the "why" reassures the public with assurances that responsibility for revolting acts (going over to the enemy side) or atrocious ones (setting bombs) falls outside the norms, that it is a pathology and, moreover, that it is "treatable."

In the wake of a number of attacks and violent incidents that occurred in France whose terrorist nature the state tried to mask until the flagrant *Charlie Hebdo* massacre, there evolved a medico-psycho-sociological rhetoric, the three avatars of pseudo-science and social engineering.[5]

A discourse of appeasement was constituted with the aim to fitting violence into rational frameworks. Its purpose was to banish the reality of Islamic violence from the public sphere and of rationalizing it by filtering it through three processes: through mental illness (psychiatry), through social or familial marginalization (sociology), through an indefinable sense of malaise (psycho-sociology).

Explanations Manufactured to Calm the Public

The public rhetoric of the explanation of terrorism in effect underwent three phases.

A MEDICALIZING RHETORIC

The medicalization of public life is a societal phenomenon:[6] Criminality is medicalized, scholarly failure is medicalized, the "end of life" is medicalized, daily life is medicalized. The general belief in pharmaceuticals is one of the great marks of progress in postmodern democracy. It reduces the citizen to a potential invalid who must therefore be watched over and treated.

Before medicalization there used to be imprisonment: prison for crime, even benign crimes (stealing bread in *Les Misérables*); reform school; the incarceration of the mentally vulnerable and of loose women (asylums and straitjackets). What is now termed "biopolitics" was born out of such control.

What succeeded this general rhetoric of imprisonment as social remedy was a general rhetoric of medicalization with a global outlook. As there were no other options on offer, when forced to explain "what should be done with these radicalized young people," politicians, already at sea in terms of how to explain the terrorist phenomenon, found a footing on the familiar ground of management, abetted in their efforts by the managerialization of health.[7]

After *Charlie Hebdo,* even this rhetorical remediation no longer sufficed: The publicity of the act, shattering the daily life of the French capital (as opposed to a small town), the evidence of its detailed planning, a network whose cunning workings were uncovered, complicity that extended as far as the ranks of the police, shoved the medicalizing explanation into the background. The explosion of this true urban guerrilla action made the official discourse of appeasement by way of psycho-medical explanations impossible, a denial of reality no longer plausible; the official discourse, faced with the terrorist acts of Coulibaly and his accomplices was forced to turn elsewhere for an explanation, outside the medical and toward the social.

A PSYCHO-SOCIOLOGICAL RHETORIC

The immediate effect of the large-scale attacks in France was to make us believe Islamic terrorism is "treatable." Why? Because if the first objective of the social contract is that we should live (as opposed to killing each other), its ulterior object is that we should live better, that the law of the jungle, the law of nature, should be replaced by a peaceful life and, as a bonus, a better life.

Terrorism, untreatable, brings us back to square one: where man is a wolf to man. Terror damages socialization. Medicine, short of lobotomy, offers neither cure nor treatment. The hackneyed image of a "lone wolf," adopted with a sarcastic turn by the Caliphate's propaganda and propagated uncritically by the Western media, has much to tell us about what we fear most: that our social contract is teetering on the brink of a feral return to simply staying alive.

So, in a second phase, came the explanation by way of psycho-sociologization. Whosoever is subjected to social, economic, or educational marginalization becomes a terrorist.

The earliest drafts of this theory about so-called "radicalization" surfaced ten or so years ago,[8] following on the groundwork by Israelis regarding Palestinian terrorism and in Great Britain regarding "homegrown" Islamic terrorism. The answer was marginalization.[9] In due course an explanation was added, having to do with a group effect, the so-called "bunch of guys" theory—a bunch of guys who through close and contagious friendship form a terrorist cell where one or several of them pass to action. The "bunch of guys" have four motivations in common: a sense of moral indignation in the face of the injustice of the world, a correlation between this injustice and "the war against Islam," a process of identifying the two previous motifs with some traumatic personal experience, and an entourage— the aforementioned "bunch"—that acts as an amplifier. The infernal machine would thus be set into motion.

On the police end, the machine that built urban terrorists could be identified by five markers (the New York police found four for conducting round-the-clock surveillance of 250 "hot spots"): a literal attachment to the Koran, adherence to a strict religious group, the expression of scorn toward the West, an inability to tolerate other beliefs, and the expression of radical political views. And to seal the deal, marginalization.[10]

This has been called the "process of radicalization."

Specialists, however, are not taken in by explanations intended to mollify the general public: They often cite Trotsky, according to whom if all it took to cross over to terror was poverty, the masses would be in permanent insurrection mode. In fact, a detailed study of the mechanisms of radicalization offers a list of twelve "mechanisms," but its conclusion offers this ingenuously disqualifying opinion:

No doubt, others still can be found. But we are certain that the more powerful the radicalization, the greater the number of mechanisms and the more complex their inter-relations.[11]

Clearly, nothing is to be gained by this tragi-comical psycho-sociological direction. Again, this is management, not explanation.

ENTER NARRATIVE

Since all public rhetoric needs to furnish explanations of what does not conform to social norms, a third, explanatory discourse is superimposed on the explanatory medico-psycho-sociological one: the narrative explanation, according to which every social action is driven by a "story" one tells both oneself and others, and this "story" is powerful by itself.

Accordingly, there is therefore an active and toxic narrative regarding the subjugation of Islam by the West that is amplified by the terrorists with a still stronger narrative, that of jihad, that must in turn be combatted by a counter-narrative from our anti-terrorist agencies.

The montage is simple: Potential terrorists tell each other a story about Islam that annuls History. We, therefore, must produce counterpropaganda and offer a counter-history, a counter-narrative. What the communications folks who are zealous about this ersatz 1970s literary criticism forget is that to explain how a narrative functions is not the same as explaining why it is more effective than another narrative. Structural literary analysis, from which narratology comes, is preoccupied with fiction and with lives on paper, not with realities and lives in flesh and blood: The only efficacy narratology is interested in, and that it can explain, is the virtuosity of a textual montage in itself, an imaginary efficacy.

So, recourse to "narrative" took off in the techniques of human resource management and product sales. Crossing over to jihadism is presented as the outcome of a stronger product narrative. Advertising for jihad is better made than advertising against jihad. This is a cognitive dead-end because a transcendental idea is not a material product, because while a product can be substituted for another product (and should be, in order to ensure a return on investment), not so an ideal. Some have begun noting the impasse of narrative determinism.[12] One ideal cannot be substituted for another.

Jihadism is religious. Not for sale. Not on the market.

To the medical explanation, to the psycho-sociological explanation, to the attempt at counterattack through narrative is added a religious (non-)explanation, that is, the denial of a religious explanation.

THE RELIGIOUS UNSPOKEN

Little thought is given to what is called conversion,[13] to this phenomenon of a return toward divinity and a community that has chosen to make divinity its center, to place its center at the center of the world. Clearly, to mention conversion is unsettling both for faith-based analysts who are mostly Christian and secularists who consider a religious conversion to be aberrant or abhorrent.

However, the spiritual dimension of warfare, as we are dealing here with warriors, cannot be simply cast aside. An exhaustive study has been conducted at the British War Academy on a neighboring topic, "spirituality," as a phenomenon integral to leadership—in a national defense and intelligence context.[14] Its merit is that it signals the obvious: that the Caliphate's combatants, the thousands who have left Europe or the Caucasus to turn toward the Promised Land, have by so doing become "leaders" on the ground, in inspiring others, and as such key characters in the literature of the Caliphate—those who show the path of *hegira* and of repentance[15] by adopting the language of the Caliph's martial harangue of May 2015.

Facing this religious reality, which perturbs a secular state, appears absurd to de-Christianized European populations and scandalous to American Christians, the fallback has been a political manipulation of public discourse.

An effort at explanation was undertaken to divest religion of its decisive power. First, the religious basis is acknowledged and recognized, but it is not identified as the trigger. This strategy's only goal, in the short term, in part and only for a time, is to avoid "stigmatizing" the population professing to be Muslim or that has Muslim cultural sensibilities. But a secondary effect, which ought to have been anticipated, is that if it is relegated to the sidelines, out of play, "under protection," this population will be subject to a dialectic movement of shame or resentment. Fertile ground for the Caliphate. Fertile ground for the next generation to accuse their parents for having denied and repressed their spiritual identity.

In a second phase, a unified, smooth, and painless vocabulary is put in place to accompany the strategy, marked by the neologism "Islamophobia," modeled on a definitely social "phobia," that is, "homophobia." This second instance of rhetorical manipulation consists of calling all critique of Islam a "phobia" in order to demote it to a sort of mental disorder, a poor adaptation to general social norms; and logically, to imply that any discourse that analyzes Islam by not being founded on an *a priori* acceptance of its social and political neutrality is itself a sign of phobia.

Thirdly, strong spirituality gets sidelined—and with it its extraordinary energy. Spirituality is socially acceptable only if it serves a secular interpretation according to which faith-believers are necessarily "good" citizens and if it fits into an acceptable, bland mode of socialization. But the disruptive nature of conversion, the fire that burns at the heart of spirituality—these have been silenced or snuffed.

A "light diet" discourse on spirituality's place in Western societies has suppressed from social debate the pent-up energy of conversion.

Unable to explain the terrorist act, its collective collateral effects are filed under the commonplace rhetorical umbrella of

Islamophobia.[16] The political class thus constructs a pseudo-explanation, for to explain by effects is not the same as explaining by causes. The cause is conversion; the effect may or may not be a phobia.

What is lost in the process, which these strategies ultimately hide, is the exoneration from all responsibility that religion offers. The question that is eliminated is, if being Muslim is not decisive in taking terrorist action, how is being Muslim decisive in not taking said action?

To sum up, what *is* decisive in becoming a "radicalized" extremist, and what in becoming a "moderate"?

The explanation lies elsewhere.

The Terrorist Chain of Reasoning

These explanations that draw on poverty, on marginalization and solidarity with the deprived, on narrative, on dissociation from the religious—they do not hold up in the face of facts: It is discovered suddenly, revealed suddenly, that jihadists are not necessarily imbeciles, mentally handicapped, or losers and marginalized people; instead they appear to be dutiful and studious daughters, who often eloquently explain their choice, who know how to write;[17] and if one of them says they had a dream showing them the path of the Caliphate, instead of seeing this as a sign of insanity or social malaise, it behooves us to start by reading some Islamic theological philosophy in order to understand how dreaming is a rational act of interpretation.[18]

Terrorists have been recruited into a category that has often nurtured rebellion, the middle class of educated *petit-bourgeois*,[19] who, whether they are Muslim or not, are capable of a reasoned revolt.

There are of course some small-time delinquents who become jihadists, but to present systematically all terrorists, as the media and the police do, as petty criminals, as the first, immediate, knee-jerk explanation, is counterproductive. It is also, in many cases, false or misleading. Those who have committed small offenses do not become terrorists because of it. They convert. Compounding this official deflected narrative, which refuses to admit the spiritual dimension of terrorism, no distinction is ever made by the police and the media between foot soldiers and cadres. As in any army, there are gradients of commitment and gradients of expertise, gradients in the ability to put into words why one serves. But the overarching motivation remains: conversion. It is proper to speak of "conversion," not "radicalization."

However, it is precisely on this graded ability to make a public case for one's choice, in one's own terms, that conversion acquires momentum: It leaves the private sphere to feed into the public sphere. Narrations of conversion construct a chain of reasoning, a rhetorical chain of solidarity between jihadists. This chain is not shaped by a logic of substitutions but by a logic of equivalences.[20]

This distinction between a logic of substitutions and a logic of equivalences is crucial in apprehending how conversion spreads socially. It is best tested by looking at the reverse process, de-radicalization.

To want to de-radicalize or de-indoctrinate[21] is predicated on a substitutive logic of differences, similar to the process of labor disputes where, for example, in order to resolve a crisis you might trade a particular demand for another. The management of social disputes is also based on this mechanism, which consists of separating one demand from another, to ensure that numerous diverse demands do not coagulate into a single massive and unmanageable demand, as evidenced recently in the Black Lives Matter movement. Political managers proceed by substitutions and by alternatives. It is the managerial retooling of *divide and rule*. It also leads us to consider social problems as discrete sub-problems, each one dealt with in isolation. Revolts happen when this chain of one-problem-at-a time-and-different-from-another breaks down.

Those who are managing the de-radicalization of youth want to apply this schema by offering values seen as substitutive, "offering alternatives," social "actions," and "human techniques that simply consist of talking,"[22] in order to short-circuit aggregate motivations.[23] None of this has resulted in tangible results.

Because, in contrast, the explanation of terrorism (how a caliphal soldier explains his choice to himself, how a young person might write about her own conversion) goes through an aggregate logic of equivalences: To become jihadist is not the result of a series of differences that can be substituted one for the other (I will do this rather than that, I am choosing to go to college instead of jihad, etc.). The decision is the result of a series of equivalences that the recruit constructs between his situation and similar situations, creating a chain of equivalences between himself and his companions, both real and dreamt, the revolutionary phenomenon that Sartre analyzed as "Fraternity-Terror."[24]

Barring the application of total censorship, blocking all communications, setting up a *huis clos*, putting all high school students in prison, the chain of equivalences will endure, Caliphate or no Caliphate. And it will be made up of tens of thousands of links. This is where, of course, some social media or messaging services have been instrumental: They do not serve "propaganda," they serve the act of building chains of equivalences between individuals. Insurrections happen when the chain of equivalences exceeds social control.

There is a further lesson that we can draw from these two contrasted modes of social formation, which has so far escaped anti-terrorist agencies that cling to outdated social theories. Jihadists have constructed a community of discourse. The fact is incontestable. So, the question we confront is: How do we, as a community of discourse ourselves, respond to or interact with the jihadist community of discourse? This is the subject of the following chapter.

ELEVEN

How Our Discourse on Terror Is Controlled

Caliphal terrorism has erupted brutally in our temperate lives, which are customarily only troubled by so-called humanitarian crises or "natural" catastrophes (and the occasional "airline drama"), all of which are manageable. Consequently, we attempt to manage the caliphal attacks socially, by recourse to the techniques we currently apply to other crises: marches against violence, laying wreaths and flowers, and collecting funds for assisting the afflicted. Brutality must be neutralized in the social rhetoric of crisis management.

Caliphal jihadism, however, is an irreversible intrusion into our community of discourse—taking "discourse" to mean generalized communication around rhetorical markers, words, sentences, codes, images that we have, or are told we have, in common and that allow us to recognize each other, to feel or believe that we exist as part of a community.

Human communities form communities of discourse by means of spoken words and text, but also by means of the images they send each other, of themselves and of others, and by the effects of truth and power these images create. A discourse community is like a film, with a picture track and a soundtrack that surround us and construct our social perceptions. Terrorism does not fall outside of this construct.

The Reality Factory: Sounds and Pictures

First, let us remember that terrifying images of throat-slitting are not new. The atrocity of which our discourse community is (not) aware is more than a decade old: It did not begin with the execution of the American journalist James Foley, beheaded on prime time in August 2014.[1]

It dates back to November 2004, when the first Internet slaughter took place as a reprisal by Bin Laden's organization for "the satanic treatment of the prisoners at Abu Ghraib," the military prison where American soldiers were abusing the virility of Iraqi prisoners, after the fall of Saddam Hussein in December 2003.[2]

The first person beheaded live on the Internet was Nick Berg. He was in Iraq because he thought it was an excellent career opportunity, in computers and communications—what else? Little did he imagine that he would be providing the substance for said communications, still less that he would be the first in what would turn out to be a macabre series: The American media correctly assessed his decapitation, a throat-slitting at the time, already, as an "initial violent response to the abuses committed at Abu Ghraib" and the "first public execution due to the new means" provided by the Internet.

This is proof that memory, in the area of communications, suffers from a degree of atrophy that impacts directly on a community of discourse: In August 2014 the media qualified Foley's killing as an "ominous development," forgetting that they had said the same thing ten years earlier.

It took ten years for the topic of these killings, inaccurately called decapitations, to be constituted in our discourse community, whereas the topics of the poor treatment of prisoners in Guantánamo and of interrogation techniques that were similar to torture had, on the contrary, come into coalescence. Justice became a key talking point: Why does the United States behave so unjustly toward prisoners?

By contrast the same community of discourse refuses to register the face value of decapitation images: decapitations are judiciary beheadings. In short, a social argument about the unjust treatment of enemies erased an argument about what sort of justice is at work in jihadist executions. The term *judiciary* is used here intentionally, as far as the killers are concerned, to convey the fact that the Caliphate's militants are, in their view, performing an act of justice. Our discourse community should no longer deny the eruption of this judicial violence, even if all we see of these beheadings are fragmentary and bowdlerized images that are presented and erased from viewing as "mad" or "barbaric."

In terms of the sound of violence, in 2004, the cries of "Allahu akbar" were already resounding, but in a sort of cacophony, a verbal paroxysm. Since then, the emission of the slogan has been codified in the scripted unfolding of the executions. In 2004, the soundtrack had the spontaneity of *cinéma vérité*, direct cinema, down to the static. In 2014, the soundtrack is almost post-production quality. In between these dates, the picture track and the shaky shots (hand-held camera style) of the first Internet execution have disappeared in a careful montage of actual executions. Something happened.

What happened is precisely the making of a jihadist discourse about judicial beheadings, made of images and sounds, iconic and sonic, while controls are being applied onto our community of discourse to frame any further understanding of the problem.

So, decapitations and beheadings have been taking place on-line for ten years. But who is being beheaded or, more precisely, of which beheadings is the general public aware?

For these are not just victims selected to shock Westerners; they are also, in great numbers and without videographic staging, people who happen to be in Syria, in Iraq, in Kurdistan, in the wrong place at the wrong time, who are accused of being collaborators, homosexuals, adulterers, cigarette resellers, kids, old people, in short, people living where the Caliphate governs.[3] All this is filmed with cell phones, in makeshift documentaries. You can see a kid kneeling, being caned for lying, seemingly more afraid than hurt. You can see a man, accused of taking drugs, whipped, then going on his way. Sharia law is applicable to the entire gamut of punishments, up to and including executions. We do not talk much about this in the West, we do not show the images. The execution of an ordinary guy in the middle of the bazaar or on a pedestrian street, with young men on motorbikes and women shopping for groceries, does not interest us.

These murders (or these judiciary punishments) do not belong to our discourse community. In our discourse community actions or reprisals undertaken by the so-called moderate militants—who with the judicious support of the West are on-the-ground actors— appear even less frequently. Our vision of brutality is one-way.

This is how discourse communities can perfectly shut their eyes or say "that is not true." In 2004 there were accusations that the Nick Berg video was a "fake," and that debate is still raging on the Internet. However, he *was* decapitated. On that score there is no argument. This debate regarding what is "fake" is regularly fueled by sudden confessions by so-called repentant jihadists or some who, presumably, have escaped the Caliphate. One such confession, by a "longtime member of the Caliphate," explains why the victims are so calm: They do not know what is about to happen to them next, to be exact, several "fake" executions.[4] Possible. Also possible is that these are proof of courage, but strangely "courage" is not evoked. Even this quality is done away with. This technical confession by a "fake" survivor is the last word in the "fake" debate. Which comforts our discourse community.

This long delay in realizing the innovative reality of terrorism and these recurrent debates about the "fake"-ness of the decapitations lead in fact to an anecdotal notion of the functioning of a discourse community that denies what does not enter into its sphere and rewrites its own film of reality, with a soundtrack and a picture track that entrench its clichés.

The short memory, the negation and the refusal of the real, are in fact the result of three behind-the-scenes control mechanisms in charge of structuring the tendencies of any discourse community.

The Controls of Discourse

The functioning of a discourse community, in fact, relies on three control systems: playing with the forbidden; the designation of madness; the policing of truth.[5] These three systems control the public deliberations on the subject of jihadism.

THE MEDIA PLAY WITH THE FORBIDDEN

Western civilization, to confine ourselves to it as it is directly targeted by this terrorism, celebrates the right to speech, the right to debate, the right to self-expression. Going back to the ancient Greeks, its roots are buried in a culture of spoken exchanges in broad view of communal action, a culture of rhetorical transactions. Even early Christianity was forced to tolerate the "pagan" art of oratory before exploiting its resources.[6]

And yet, of late, a whole system of laws has been established to promote and move in a specific direction, to debate and argue about demands that seem natural and imperative; this new direction consists of blocking anything that appears unbearable as an argument—for example, the laws against historic revisionism or insults of a racial or sexual nature—even if their virulence varies, depending on whether it is a matter of law (in the case of genocide, in some countries) or of social perception (in the case of the variants deemed acceptable on American campuses). The control system too can be openly attacked (the USA), mocked (France), interiorized to such a degree that a layer of silence can prevent the denunciation of crimes (sexual slavery within the migrant milieu in Great Britain), but it is, nevertheless, in place.

In short, we liberate, we constrain. We rejoice in interdiction, whether we are on the side of those who intentionally infringe on taboo or on the side of those who demand its application. Interdiction creates a link between things said, which the verb *interdict* denotes, composed as it is of *inter* and *dict*, from the Latin verb *dicere*, to say. This linking exercises control over the discourse community.

To illustrate this point, the beheading videos: When beheading videos, even censored, are shown to the public, what happens is a game of interdiction. Because the media, by putting a recent taboo on view, that of public execution, are playing with an interdiction; by editing the images, they apply self-censorship, thus entering into a perverse game with the interdiction: to show, not to show, a little, only so much, to stop *in extremis*, to reprise. Everything is shown, other than the crucial moment that justifies the event, in order not to "offend, disturb."

The result of this game is to prevent all true discussion: A rhetorical transaction does not take place. The manipulation of brutal and violent images by the media is the equivalent of the laws that forbid questioning the genocide committed by Germany. In other words, control.

A "NORMAL" SOCIETY NEEDS A PLACE FOR MADNESS

Every discourse community, to ensure its handle on events, needs "the world," reality, so it must designate the limits where its domain ends and "madness" begins. Public deliberation constantly oscillates between two assignations: For example, one might assert that an argument is ridiculous and affirm that another is, on the contrary, serious. Small rhetorical banalities that are nonetheless upheld by a system of control assigning them their places as normal and as insane.

In the old days, the insane were placed in asylums. Designations were made clearly, with walls and straitjackets, as to where insanity belonged. How were the insane treated in those days? They were jailed, given shock treatment, or they were laughed at. The madman was a source of mirth. The child with Down syndrome was a source of laughter. A woman lawyer, around

1920, would elicit a smirk.[7] An educated African elicited laughter. They were all perceived as modulations of the unreasonable, as inopportune aberrations in the observance of established norms.

Things are less cut and dried these days for demarcating normal and deviant territory, in part due to transformations in diagnostic processes and medical practices inspired by business management: For example, depressed individuals are no longer potential madmen to be placed in "asylums" but clients of pharmaceutical products.[8]

At least they were, until the apparition of the Caliphate's jihadism.

The Caliphate's propagandistic and terrifying montages suddenly allowed the reestablishment of a rigid designation of the pathological: The Caliphate lets us delineate a zone of madness on the mental and physical maps of our vision of the world.

We can consult the geographical map: There exists a demented territory, around Mosul.[9] For our discourse community, therefore, the terrorist is the new figure of madness. And the Caliphate is the new domain of the insane.

So there is a normal zone, a place of truth, of reason, of open debate, of transactions between individuals, where we recognize that to be able to speak is to be able to reason; and also, as an ever-spreading stain, the land of the Caliphate, and beyond it the cyberland of jihadism. A zone "to close off" or to treat chemically, if we could find the means of doing so, that is inhabited by delirious madmen. When the caliph delivered his very eloquent sermon in the course of which the Caliphate was founded, in a succession to Muhammad, as if he were perfectly entitled to believe and to reason by Koranic theory, the reaction was to burst out laughing, as one might in the face of a madman. This is the tenor of reactions one can read on innumerable Internet forums.

This reaction is not new: At the beginning of the eighth century, Saint John of Damascus, descendant of a line of noble functionaries who served the Mohammedan occupants, refused to convert when Caliph Omar II inflicted punitive measures against Christians in the Orient. He then composed the first Christian book about the Koran and Islam.[10] In it, we find this sentence, a forecast of derisions to come: "This book is full of absurdities that it would behoove one to laugh at." "Laughable, ridiculous, derisory," are the key qualifications of the pamphlet. Whoever has seen the entirety of the new caliph's proclamation ceremony, has listened to the sermon, has observed the auditorium of the faithful can come away with only one conclusion: This is extremely serious.

All discourse communities function by designating a line that divides the normal from the insane, knowing that to confirm the soundness of their own discourse, they must designate the person speaking that is a "madman." The person who is "off base." Persons that are feared, laughed at, while "vulnerable" individuals are removed from their vicinity; and a line is drawn. We think, by so doing, we control what disturbs *us*—for it is we who are, in reality, the disturbed: This social rhetoric asserts that if we begin to want to lift the controls and to actually speak to the madman, in this instance the Caliphate, to establish deliberation beyond the dividing line designating the normal and the pathological, it is we, ourselves, who would be at risk of madness.

This is the consequence of interdicting public deliberation as the second control requires.

THE TRUTH POLICE

This explains the third constraint imposed on public deliberation: the capital role of the journalistic process of "commentary" in the truncated shows of executions or attacks. The media impose a commentary over these images in order to substitute themselves in and to function as a truth police.

The mediatized habit of commentary over politicians' speech at the very instant they are speaking (replacing speech with "over-speech") has become such the disciplinary norm in the profession that it is applied even more seamlessly to the essential taboo, that of human sacrifice. It has reached the point that there is commentary over the words being spoken by an individual about to be executed, as though the words he speaks were not enough. The truth of the Caliphate is inaudible because if it were to speak for itself, it would mean dissolving the dividing line drawn by discourse control between terrorists and moderate, "integrated" Muslims.

So long as the media carry on representing, in the manner

of a strip-tease, the sounds and images of brutal acts, titillating our desire for the forbidden, playing with our desire to hurl invectives at "these jihadist madmen" and to play at truth police, the Caliphate's communications strategists will continue to film and to feed our shared fantasies. The Caliphate and its communications strategists have fully grasped that they need to feed our machinery of control, and this is exactly what they do, with great acumen, so we find ourselves unable to go beyond the images and the sounds and ask the fundamental question, which is that of the apparition of a "people," the people of the Caliphate, whose reality we refuse to acknowledge, and who will endure whatever may happen to the Islamic State as a territorial entity.

TWELVE

Jihadist Populism

With the "homegrown" terrorist comes a political phenomenon occulted by the rhetoric of normal politics, relegated to management norms: a free people and the voluntarist individual at its foundation. The individual, the people: two concrete sources of the otherwise abstract notion of "the will of the people."[1]

French or German "homegrown" terrorists, whether soldiers of the Caliphate in the Orient or its partisans within Western borders, are not only an insane form of politics, as one would have you believe: They are actually the manifestation of a "people" and of a phenomenon of voluntarism.

Jihadist Voluntarism

All public discourse—the upshot of previous analyses—aims at obfuscating this question of the "homegrown" terrorist or jihadist: Isn't terrorism, in fact, a reappearance of the political individual who makes a decision, and who, by adhering to others of the same persuasion, forms a people?

A willing and able individual adds himself to other individuals, whose will and ability to act become "terrorism" and who, aligned under a political credo, form a revolutionary avant-garde—the Caliphate. To use Leninist language, the Caliphate can be considered an "avant-garde": It is doctrinaire in its discourse, organized into committees, involved in combat, ready to sow terror among the enemies of its class and is therefore advancing the message of a global revolution. That this avant-garde happens to be Muslim in no way changes the system.

This description is obviously not that of the official rhetoric, the national media, or the confused political overseers.

The official discourse about terrorists affirms that terrorists are manipulated from the outside, that they are not a manifestation of the people. They are agents of an entity that is not "us." They have exited the "us": They are unbalanced, indoctrinated, "radicalized," lost young persons, newly minted nationals threatened with the loss of nationality. In short, marginals of the "us." All deliberate political voluntarism is denied them.

This official rhetoric is a denial of reality. It refuses to take into consideration that terrorism is a form of politics and the (unexpected) appearance of a people.

This rhetoric of political class and mediatized relays is in its essence managerial, it considers people as a human resource to be assigned performance goals; it is a manipulation in order not to confront reality, that is to say for maintaining said reality inside fixed processes (realistically, elections serve as road maps to the performance of parties). The managerial approach must preserve the myth of the managerial cadres of normal politics: Neither the political individual nor the political people can or should exist. The popular will is "general," generalized, it is not at the level of the voluntarist individual. Such is the ambient doxa.

Each time that, notwithstanding the management protocols in place, a resurgence of this kind occurs, necessarily violent because it is repressed, the political method for managing the problem adopts four modes of intervention: affirming that the state alone owns the use of force; accentuating security measures; holding a moralizing discourse on good and evil, the normal and the pathological; and the recourse to prevention.

Never is the fundamental question on the table: And what if this is the people, and, from the people, the politicized individual (the very subject of democracy) who is there, saying "no"?

Here is what is concealed in this desire to treat terrorism as an exception to normal politics, to treat it as an ailment: This rhetoric denying terrorism as a form of politics is a rhetoric that denies terrorism as a powerful form of populism.[2]

Characteristics of Jihadist Populism

Caliphal jihadism comprises all the attributes of any strong populism, the kind that drives revolutions.

AFFIRMING THE TRUE PEOPLE

In the first place, jihadism radically divides political society in two: not into rich and poor, haves and have-nots, the country as a legal entity and the country in reality; across a spectrum of formulations, from the far right to the far left. Rather, it divides it on a different scale, a separation among those who live in immanence and those who live according to a transcendent belief, miscreants and believers.

Western societies have eliminated the populist potential of religious transcendence but, like any potential, this populism is actively ready to rebound. And so it has, under the auspices of the Islamic Caliphate.

Eloquent appeals to a holy war, in the Caliphate's publications, are an appeal to the people. The Caliphate's appeal posits on the basis of transcendence a *radical* split between the bad part of the people (the elites, the rich, the bought and sold, miscreants in everyday materialism) and the best part of the people, the one that resists, decides, commits. That the conflict is religious changes little about the Caliphate's populism, except that our political discourse, which is essentially secular without admitting all its consequences, refuses to integrate religious factors into forms of populism that intellectual habits instinctively assign to what since the American and French revolutions we have come to label as "the people." Other than this "people," there also exists what religion refers to as "the people of God." How both "peoples" may co-exist remains a conundrum, thrown under a sharp light by Islamic fundamentalism, be it of the Muslim Brothers' form or that of the Caliphate.

By way of proof, here is an excerpt from the French magazine *Dār al-Islām* with the following injunction:

> This cursed rag that is *Charlie Hebdo* made fun of Jesus the Messiah and his mother Mary more than once; what did Christians who pretend to love Christ and his mother to the point of adoring them outside of Allah do? Nothing! The Jews in their Talmud insult them in the worst way. How could Christians, in France and elsewhere, accept to be governed by this band of vipers? We call on Christians to stop accepting Jewish domination and to accept the only religion that defends what is sacred, the religion of all the prophets, the only true religion: Islam.[3]

It doesn't get any clearer. There exist two peoples. One willing to falter in its convictions, manipulated by the powerful and the influential, the other affirming its conviction and showing the way of insurrection. Populism is the name assigned to the fissure between the true and the false people, it points a finger at it, reveals it as evidence. The technique of South American populisms.

REJECTING CLASS HIERARCHIES

Here we see another rhetorical populism at work, the favorite theme of betrayal by the elites:

> We end this preface to the second issue of *Dār al-Islām* by making it clear that this magazine is addressing neither researchers nor miscreant journalists nor pseudo-Muslims who want to

study the Islamic State and who will attack us anyway even if our spelling and our syntax are perfect. We are also not addressing the pseudo-partisans of jihad who think that they are doing something for their religion by spending their nights on social networks. *Dār al-Islām* is only a tool for inciting to *hegira* and to jihad and a modest contribution from our francophone brothers who live in the Caliphate and who see this state being built around them on the blood of their brothers.[4]

The formulas found here are identical to South American populisms, for example: the denunciation of arrangements among elites against the betrayed innocence of the people at the bottom, the perverse power of the press against the common sense of the people, false allies of the cause of the people against its true defenders. The young Australian Jake who volunteered for a suicide attack, "wishing for martyrdom," in the fighting of February 2015 explained that he preferred death to living in the "rot and corruption of Australian society," a typically populist argument:

The reality of democracy became clear to me, to place in the mind of the people the idea of freedom and convince them that they are a free people while oppressing them behind the scenes. On top of this the Western world throws celebrities and false reality into the spotlight to distract the people from what is really going on in the world, hence the widespread political ignorance among Westerners.[5]

You couldn't put it any better. The Caliphate resolutely takes the side of the people: In its literature it rejects the distinction, common in high Arab-Muslim philosophy, between popular persuasive effects and persuasive effects reserved for an elite versed in the mysteries of interpretative analysis. It rejects all elitism, specifically the social typology set up by Averroës:

> There is a hierarchy of human natures with regard to all that is assent: Some men assent as a result of demonstration; others assent as a result of the effect of dialectic argument; still others assent as a result of the effect of rhetorical argument.[6]

The Caliphate rejects the notion of a hierarchy of human natures where the capacity for persuasion through reason is concerned. It does away with these distinctions to assert that no hierarchy exists in assenting to divine law—which explains why Caliphate publications and videos cleverly blend analyses, interpellations, biographies, leaflets, Koranic citations, and citations from philosophies and doctors of the faith. The people of God is made up of equals. A populist argument.

DESIGNATING THE ENEMY

The third characteristic of populism is its designation of an Other: an enemy. There needs to exist a declared or labeled enemy: "the rich" in South America, sometimes "intellectuals" (a favorite target of the Perón faction and of Maoism), "profiteers" (Leninism). This is the operative device in the *Dār al-Islām* quotation above with its attack against "Jews." Shocking? In fact, this designation in France belongs to a traditional political language of populism; it is simply repressed today because of the real risk of criminal punishment. But it has often served to contrast "real French people" with the rest, the non-natives or manipulators, on the right as on the left. So it is a potentially efficient rhetorical code, especially in France: The propagandists of the Caliphate know how to exploit a rift.

Whence this trait: to denounce, to unmask, to destroy those who collaborate with the enslavement of the true people. The literature of the Caliphate commonly talks about "palace scholars," referring to Muslim intellectuals who, from the comfort of an existence among the miscreants, serve their Western masters. A caricature? Populisms must caricature their adversaries in order to highlight their salient traits.

A feature of this type of designation of the enemy is, in fact, to accentuate any rift by amplifying antagonisms. The purpose is a polarization.

It is worth noting that the English-language equivalent of *Dār al-Islām, Dābiq,* does not use the same anti-Jewish cleavage argument but a different argument that touches a sensitive chord in England: that of the United Kingdom's military and financial alignment with its American "master," employing a subtle comparison with "subjugated" Japan. The effect is less brutal, but the effort at designating an enemy that is abusing "the people" is evident.

The aim is to place the individual before a binary choice.

LIBERATING THE EXCLUDED

A fourth element of populist rhetoric is the argument of exclusion. In populism, it is acknowledged that the demands proffered by "the people" to those denounced as "bad" are the fruit of and a sign of an exclusion. The "excluded" make their demand from a place of exclusion. This theme turns up in all terrorist confessions. Reading terrorist messages, a corollary theme emerges: the sense of impotence in the face of the power of the "corrupt," the sense of aggravated injustice. This argument of exclusion, however, now undergoes a rhetorical twist at the hands of counterterrorism services and the media: The explanation is given that one reason for the passage to terrorism is social exclusion. We noted earlier that if most of the time the facts discredit such an assertion when this argument is employed by agencies, terrorists themselves turn it into a celebration of the power drawn from exclusion: These are the new "damned of this earth," who, lifting their heads, affirm that a rotten and corrupt political world has excluded them and therefore that those excluded must be assembled into a terrifying force. In speaking heedlessly of "exclusion," we are serving jihadists what they want us to say. The conversion, jihad, is an appeal to the excluded. Not in the socio-economical, managerial sense of social exclusion, but in the mystical sense of a return to true values, a reconstitution, an inclusive gathering of the "people of God."

A Spontaneous People

A traditional theme of populism is that "the people" rise up spontaneously. There are, of course, way stations and relays but without this spontaneous reaction, from the bottom up, from the street, a populist action can have no engine.

The theory of populism goes so far as to assert that "the people" takes its true form and reality within this double constraint of grassroots spontaneity and self-organized relays. Terrorism too: the ideal of an absolute people, taking shape through relays and acting on the basis of individual initiatives. You can therefore become a jihadist spontaneously, on your own, but in a movement toward others, a community.

When the Caliphate claims responsibility for a strike, it is redundant to say that retroactive recognition is what allows the Caliphate to "project its power" as a *modus operandi*:[7] In populist action it is the base that acts, without needing to receive precise orders from above. There is no chain of command: The motivation bypasses the chain of command. It is understandable that police work needs to establish what lawyers call "causation." But it is a political mistake to wish causation into a terrorist act. Claiming an attack that is the outcome of voluntarism need not therefore be immediate, direct or explanatory, on the part of the Caliphate, though we might wish it were, in accordance with our judiciary logic.

The Caliphate knows how to play with our expectations of causation, and our legalistic view of war, and our inability to grant individuals freedom of decision. For instance, in the case of an attack against a gas factory in France in the Isère region on

June 26, 2015, we first had to wait for an issue of *Dābiq* to come out, in which the Caliphate listed the attack, "in the Crusader city of Lyon," on its front page as a "defense of the Caliphate," and this on July 14, the national day of France. However, in anticipation of this release, on July 7 a video in Turkish from *İslam Devleti* (Islamic State) had showed a Francophone militia member and scenes of a factory explosion. Only a close scrutiny of the Caliphate's prolific propaganda brought it up. In the third place, another fact not highlighted by the media, nor apparently by the public prosecutor, took an investigative eye to pinpoint: The target of the attack, Air Products, is a company that holds 25 percent of the Saudi company AHG, the principal provider of civil and military industries in Saudi Arabia, a designated enemy of the Caliphate.[8] The terrorist, who worked there, was not told to attack Air Products. He came to that conclusion on his own. But the Caliphate's media arm was quick to create a frame. The relationship between center and agent is therefore dialectical. It is not linear, as in a chain of command.

Revolutionary populism is indeed a dialectic between individual willingness and social formation in motion. In other words, we would need to apply to jihadism the modes of analysis associated with the "new social movements." Like them, it too is a transversal struggle.

That this "people" is normalized through religion does not change any facet of the process. It is time this was acknowledged, because what it points to is a movement whereby the world is undergoing a populist re-enchantment of the most radical kind—and not electoral "populism" as it is tritely presented in the media. An accumulation of spontaneous actions and group actions, gradually bringing about a movement of collective consciousness. And this movement, expanding, becomes a constitutive logic for "the true, the good people," a brutal resurgence of "the people" that takes on an irresistible, political shape and that, where the enemy is concerned, translates into a radical hostility.[9]

THIRTEEN

A Radical Hostility

The political philosopher Carl Schmitt concluded his *Theory of the Partisan*, composed in the early 1960s, with these premonitory words:

> Who can prevent unexpected new types of enmity from arising in an analogous, but ever more intensified way, whose fulfillment will produce unexpected new forms of a new partisan?

And he summed up his work, which was contemporaneous with the events in Algeria, with an invitation to intellectuals to reflect on the subject:

> The theoretician can do no more than verify concepts and call things by name. The theory of the partisan flows into the question of the concept of the political, into the question of the real enemy and of a new *nomos* of the earth.[1]

Nomos defines the integrated territory of a given community, at once concrete in the motions of daily life, abstract by the internalization of laws, mental by the realities memorialized, emotional by devotion to values. This specialized concept, *nomos*, allows us to think of the essence of politics not in abstract terms (constitution, universal values, etc.) but as a territory that is physical and mental, legal and spiritual, yet always perceived by individuals as a deeply rooted sense of belonging to a place. The glossary confusion in naming the Caliphate and the strategies of refusal whose simultaneous lack of efficacy and naiveté have been detailed in the course of the previous chapters attest to this.

A Guerrilla Force of Partisans

The Caliphate bids us to weigh Schmitt's political premonition and rise to the challenge, that is, to consider the Caliphate as a new form of politics, whatever happens to the Islamic State.

A new hostility terrifies, but it first terrifies the language of our discourse community. We must put an end to the sensationalist rhetoric of the media and professional politicians and name the phenomenon precisely, a Caliphate, its actors "soldiers and partisans" and its actions "war and guerrilla warfare."

The political class and media outlets resist when faced with naming the hostility: because in our societies violence is framed by law (for every form of violence there is a corresponding crime) and is reduced to an explanatory rhetoric (sociology, psychology, etc.) with a view to relegating it to the dominant ideology of human groups as objects of management (prevention, incarceration, reintegration).

But when true violence erupts, with its soundtrack and its picture track, its sacrificers and its victims, its appeals and its harangues, its horror and its strange heroism, its ideals and its prestige, a trouble in naming develops: We are deprived of the exact words for expressing it and reduced to employing a devalued glossary, faced with the unbearable defiance of this new violence, which to us seems like a return to "barbarism," to the natural state of "savages," before there was a social contract, or to dark, so-called "medieval" comportments. Public discourse falls back on a facile solution: The new hostility, unnamable, of jihadism and of the Caliphate belongs neither to our time nor to our space.

It is precisely at this juncture that it can be fruitful to reflect about subversive war as it can help us understand what is crucial[2] with regard to our own discourse community: How are the Caliphate jihadists operating on our national soil, in our time and in our space, implanting a new form of proximity, partisan terrorism?

"The Soldier in Uniform Target of the Modern Partisan"[3]

The Caliphate's propaganda is clear: Every representative in uniform belonging to the state where the jihadist lives must be killed, until the takeover of the territory or its capture by the Caliphate's regular army. For the Caliphate, that half of Europe that was under Islamic rule at some stage is occupied by enemies—

miscreants and their allies and servants, "moderate Muslims." The police forces and the deployed army are forces of occupation. Consequently, jihadists must resist the occupier by practicing guerrilla warfare and by becoming partisans. Recent attacks are acts of resistance against occupiers.[4]

As the Caliphate's propaganda instructs, every object must be made into a weapon.

So, not only does the partisan, until the day of the attack, disappear in the anonymity of crowds, but he can make the weapon disappear in the banality of everyday utensils—a knife, a hatchet, a cleaver, even a motor vehicle.[5]

A partisan "blends into the background," this is the *modus operandi* of partisan warfare. Utensils facilitate disappearance. Even groups can blend into our cities. Cities are in essence producers of anonymity. "Lone wolf," the media intoned for two years, but were they not forgetting, if they were to examine the metaphor, that wolves travel in packs and can hide under cover?[6] They can attack alone. But the pack is around, is real on the ground, and on the terrain of the Internet.[7] Cities are the new deep forests of previous guerrillas.

It is therefore a battle of irregulars against regulars, of soldiers with no uniform who melt into the urban landscape against regular soldiers who turn into targets—the attacks targeting members of the military in France, in Great Britain, in the United States, in Canada, are conclusive.[8] The essential is this: Every regular soldier is a target for the partisan. From then on, the language of hostility changes, because the frontline is within proximity, traversing in multiple ways our *nomos*, to speak as Schmitt might: To say terrorist "act" is not enough, we must say "attack by a political guerrilla."

The act, said to be an act of terror committed by a partisan, is indeed a political act, an act that is aligned with a party. The party of God, in its own eyes. The party of the Caliphate. We are not dealing with criminal terrorism[9] but with political warfare in the most caustic sense of the term—a war that targets the very nature of politics as we have known it.

The Caliphate has this in common with revolutionary organizations of yesteryear, that it demands and instills total belligerence in its partisans as an absolute requisite.

A regular soldier, a combatant, need not agree with or disagree with the politics of the government that enjoins him or her to fight. Soldiers fulfill their duty as it is asked of them. If there is a personal political commitment on their part, beyond the service owed, it is not decisive: Loyalty to the state and political neutrality are the rule.[10]

Jihadist partisans, on the other hand, are integrally a part of a grand plan that goes beyond them and that at the same time elevates them. They align themselves with a politics. We can pathologize, psychologize, and sociologize all we want in order to "explain radicalization"; the fact is all these Caliphate partisans are given over, body and soul, to an ideal that has made them other and, in their own eyes, better than themselves. Their loyalty exceeds the duty owed. Their vital sacrifice is not of the order of the possible but of the order of the certain.

The principle characteristic of complete devotion to a political line, one moreover that is populist in its dynamic and, furthermore, that pertains to a transcendence, is that you can adhere to it by yourself: A young person who decides to join the jihad converts to a doctrine. The strongest convictions are those acquired by oneself, and the biographies of jihadists are here to prove it, as previously noted.[11]

When we are confronted with this reemergence of the political partisan, and therefore a political war, we are mentally disarmed, and we seek comfort in amorphous explanations in the face of what is the fundamental basis of religious phenomena, here transferred to political action: The sacred does not distinguish itself from the profane by a difference in size, greater or lesser on the scales of codes or values, but by a difference in nature. Partisans are aligning themselves on a level that falls outside of our quantifiables.

"The Partisan Succeeds in Adapting to the Technical-Industrial Environment"

Schmitt had Guevara and Castro in mind, but the formula holds. Aside from the innumerable means of locomotion at the disposal of today's partisans, exponentially augmented by the outrageous motorization of our way of life and the ease with which these means can be appropriated (legally or illegally), not counting the dense networks of air, rail, and maritime connections, the technicalization of partisan warfare has added to its panoply the Internet and e-communication[12]—in addition to spatial mobility, there is now virtual mobility whose speed is unrivaled. And we have seen how wisely the Caliphate, and before it, Al-Qaeda, has exploited the Internet. When, thoughtlessly, we are told that this or that terrorist is a lone wolf, the response is, of course he is, it is what allows him to be mobile, quick, not identifiable, until he slips up, is exposed in the digital field, and sets off a surveillance alert.

A guidebook for jihadists that appeared in 2015 is explicit and detailed regarding the methods for "guerrilla warfare" to be put into action in the "heart of Europe": One or two naive but practical details, on which the great wits of the Internet pounced, in no way invalidate the gravity of the book, for example in regard to the preparation of bombs, survival methods, familiarization with personal defense, etc.[13]

And like the partisans of the old days, or of today, in southeast Asia or South America, who navigated networks of thickets and undergrowth and ditches, so too the Caliphate's partisans can use networks in which to hide themselves by dint of the Internet jungle.[14]

The partisan is mobile, quick, supple, and technically capable as never before in a subversive war. Guerrilla actions on national soil are a formidable expansion of the Caliphate's "directorate of operations," whose efficiency is now recognized (this delivers another marker of statehood).[15]

"The Absolute Aggressivity
of a World-Revolutionary Ideology"

Here we must weigh each element of the Schmittian definition: absolute aggressivity, world-revolutionary ideology.

The political class and the media, however, want to forget that the Caliphate's aggressive posture is presented as a response to an aggression.

Defense against "the Crusaders" (a generic propaganda term) and against "palace scholars" (those subtle minds that offer Westerners a pleasant interpretation but stray from Islam) and against apostates and idolaters (Arab regimes). The partisan takes on the defense of what he believes in: This is a legitimate defense, and he will plead not guilty, like Tsarnaev.[16]

We are the aggressors.

But this defensive posture is transformed into an aggressive posture, because in the course of the defense, the partisan perceives that the action in which he is engaged must be absolute. By principle, a defensive posture is never absolute: It is relative to an attack. An aggressive posture can be absolute: It need set no endpoint, apart from the destruction of the adversary and one's own destruction, if need be. Here, there is no question, as in a military action, of moving from the defensive to the offensive while calculating where to stop; military calculation can therefore be aligned with the political calculation that is eluding it. Here there is only a push toward the absolute, which considers the triumph of the partisan's beliefs to mean a total destruction of the adversary. A terrorist does not proceed by half-measures. The world is to be revolutionized, in other words entirely repositioned to the place it ought to have been: in Islam.

The Caliphate's irresistible expansion in the theater of operations and in the terrain of guerrilla warfare is proof.[17] Schmitt refers to the "telluric" character of the passage from defensiveness to absolute aggression, in short the desire for absolute control over territory, over the Earth.

Does this "telluric" process come as a surprise? In fact this is how French revolutionary ideas were spread across Europe—with German, Dutch, and English deputies demanding that the French invade their tyrannical regimes; and this invasive proselytism was the cause of such an insurrectional fear in the United States that the first emergency anti-terrorism law, long before the Patriot Act, was established by George Washington against "the French." Tellurism was also the mainspring of Hitlerism in its appeal to "European" youth, placing the defense of race above nationalisms. And think of the Soviets spreading beyond the frontiers of the USSR with the Internationale and the Comintern. All, "telluric" processes of globalization.

Necessarily, this turn to absolutism means that territories, as we know them, cease to exist, limits are abolished and geographic entities disappear under the impetus of the globalization of the struggle and the absolute coincidence sought between the Earth and the strength of this conviction.

Here the term *terrorist* applies exactly: A "terrorist" takes on the defense of his territory, which is in fact all the Earth, by this mutation of the defensive posture into absolute aggression. And his first duty is the restitution of the territory in which he lives, where he exerts his actions as a partisan, to the source that guarantees him, the Caliphate.

"A Transformation of the Concepts of War, the Enemy," and the Partisan

A series of ideas then come into alignment concerning "partisan warfare,"[18] political war, enemies and radical hostility, what Schmitt called "a successive transformation," a deep metamorphosis.

Partisan warfare is the term for a modern form of popular warfare. Clausewitz, when he wrote *On War*, had two contemporaneous models of irregular warfare in mind: the Spanish popular insurrection of 1809 and the call to insurrection by the Prussian king in 1813.[19] Their model, though, is that of the French enemy: the nation in arms. Based on the French revolutionary model, the concept of the partisan as the irregular defender of territory is put into place. If, as Clausewitz asserts, war is a political instrument, partisan warfare (which used to be called "guerrilla war") is now integrated into a rationalist schema of warfare.

Moreover, there is an ethical consequence to such theorizing about this military novelty as we start by observing that war by partisans is war by other means, but above all for other reasons. Then we are forced to recognize, in those that are not soldiers by profession and are therefore acting out of a "natural and blind impulse" of hatred toward the occupier, their capacity for "courage and talent," in the past the sole preserve of the regularly trained military. The partisan acquires ethical value.

The notion of "military valor," of heroism, has therefore been expanded. This is precisely the case with regard to Caliphate propaganda, which in its English, French, German, Russian,[20] Turkish[21] publications celebrates the heroic figures of partisans fallen in the fields of honor, valiant deaths.

This "deep" metamorphosis cannot go unacknowledged.

A War without Rules

Marxism-Leninism furnishes the Caliphate not with a model but with an explanatory schema that goes beyond partisan warfare and redefines the terms of a "political war."

Schmitt reminds us in effect that Lenin, reading Clausewitz and with an eye to world revolution, made a distinction between war games and war itself.

Interstate wars are war games. As with all games, they have rules and a field of play. The enemy military leaders all speak the same language, often from the same books. What we have is regulated hostility.

Opposed to this, in the Leninist conception war is absolute hostility. It knows neither rules, nor conventions, nor limits. Class struggle is concretized in this absolute form of war where everything is allowed since nothing is a means to anything other than the destruction of the standing order of things.

What war-as-game calls armistice, the suspension of arms, the exchange of prisoners even, respect for the rights of combatants, it all means nothing other than—and Lenin notes this—using these rules when they are useful and only when they are useful. This analysis is directly applicable to the Caliphate, to jihadism, and it explains the disarray of the regular powers in the face of torture, piracy on the open seas, guerrilla warfare, but also the rapid deployment of communication and networks, and finally the redoubtable military efficacy of the Caliphate.[22] From a military strategy perspective, the Caliphate practices an offensive without respite, an offensive at all costs.[23] Western strategists have even applied the term *surge*, which was coined in Iraq in 2007 and taken up again in Afghanistan in 2009, to describe the Caliphate's intensification of military effort on the ground within the framework of a counter-offensive.[24] When a fabricated word—fabricated to qualify one's own efforts in a laudatory manner—is adopted to describe an adverse strategy in a military context, the rhetorical transfer is either an avowal of confusion or a desire to assimilate the adversary's game into a framework and a language that one controls and then to understand the strategy. The Caliphate actually does not implement a regulated *surge* but an impenitent offensive that has always taken place with troops on the ground. It is not playing the game.

In response, the communications strategy of the military forces involved function in a mode of rhetorical disinformation by minimizing risks before the fact and exaggerating risks afterwards: The communication strategist pushes the theme "*Daesh retreats*" and that of minimizing objectives ("a second-rate refinery"), which, as soon as it is belied by dazzling victories becomes "a key refinery falls to IS"; this communications strategy has ultimately proven unproductive.[25] But after first deriding the Caliphate troops, military analysts were forced to admit the reality and validity of a strategy based on a constant ground offensive, the efficacy of military training, and the conduct in combat of the Caliphate's soldiers:

> Fully determined in their tactics, their movements, the cadence of their shots, precise, discipline in battle. Their message: We know what we're doing, and we're good at it.[26]

This war, in its double dimension as a guerrilla war in its external operations and as a conventional war in the domestic theater, is the kind of war we believed had been eliminated after the nineteenth century: a war of conquest,[27] and a war of conquest without an endgame, without an announced limit.

One consequence of this turnaround in the situation is the military's realization that the Islamic State is a state. It is the military that dared shatter the political taboo[28] by recognizing that a war with no rule other than that of a constant offensive, a political war incorporating all available forms, culminates in the creation of an incontestable political reality.[29] It is symptomatic that while pages of strategy have been filled on the question of "failed states"[30] (the *de facto* terrain of the Caliphate's conquests in the Middle East and, who knows, perhaps in the Balkans and the Caucuses as well), next to nothing has been written on the formation of this "proto-state," whose model is likely to be emulated if it is vanquished in its present form.[31]

By the same token, recourse by strategists to the notion of a "hybrid war" (with regular or irregular operations) can fulfill a wish for game (in Leninist terms) or for formalization (in Clausewitzian terms), but it has the advantage of allowing that the political war waged by the Caliphate is

> a formal structured organization that plans at multiple levels of war in a conventional sense and elects at times, sometimes simultaneously, to employ multiple styles of warfare as specialized and combined means.[32]

Amid this amphigory, a key word: "styles." To say "styles" after saying "formal organization" is to concede that the Caliphate is ahead in the game: plasticity.

Another consequence is to cast doubt on the validity of the discussion, the strategic doctrine, on what is called "moral asymmetry."

Indeed, international law imposes legal rules on states as much in the decision to fight a war as in the conduct of the hostilities.[33]

The Caliphate, however, with its regular soldiers and its irregular partisans, does not believe, rightly in its own eyes, that it needs to respect these rules or even to consider them as anything other than supplementary means invented by the miscreants to ensure the enslavement of its faithful. A state bound by international law cannot respond by repression against the accomplices and families of the partisans, nor by a war of annihilation targeting enemy populations, nor by the execution of its prisoners. It operates under a moral asymmetry that stacks the deck in this game of war, given that one of the players rejects the rules, fabricates its own pieces, and constantly redraws the board.

This moral asymmetry is rarely highlighted by the counterpropaganda of the states engaged against terrorism: We fail to explain to the public a pivotal dimension of the conflicts.

The "Fore-Aft" Strategy

For a military map that is outdone in the theater of operations in the Levant, there is the map moved forward by recruitment or by the apparition of a partisan. We are "aft" in a caliphal war, whose "fore" is Iraq and Syria.

With the deployment of the French army on national territory,[34] the anti-Caliphate war is now unfolding within and without:[35] domestically as an internal theater of operations, outside the borders as normal external operations. Germany is following suit. Others have, timidly, or will, less so as partisan warfare intensifies.

The Caliphate has succeeded, therefore, in transforming Western national territories into the "aft" of the battlefields of the Levant, with all the consequences that this entails, for example accrued surveillance of the population, denunciations among the French, and public alerts.

We have admitted, therefore, that this war is a war of conquest and that enemy soldiers, while we refuse to call them by this name, are operating right here.

This unacknowledged notion of a fore and aft game at last explains how, in the attribution of the attacks, analysts often go no further than a fallacious explanatory code: Instead of quibbles as to whether or not it is really the Islamic State claiming responsibility for an assassination, we need to admit that the retroactivity of the authorship of attacks, the recognition of attribution "without explicit links," is the outcome of there being a fore and aft strategy:[36] The Caliphate is operating outside of caliphal territory, that is, in the West, the way that a Resistance would.

It follows that what preoccupies strategists, namely the "power ratio," is profoundly upset: The traditional qualitative rapport (a tenant of an asymmetric war) collapses before the new qualitative relationship introduced by the dazzling and fruitful apparition of a radical political war.

We are on the "aft" of armies that are present, and we live in a territory marked for attack by a radical hostility emanating from a proto-state or a "state of exception" that, were it to experience some setbacks and even a defeat, will have engendered an aspiration that will not disappear but will remain alive.

A Radical Differend

Caliphal Islamic terrorism is characterized by a generalized, polymorphous, and limitless hostility. It is beyond all measure. Such is its form.

By its harangues, its appeals, its hagiographies, its rites, and its accounts, the Caliphate has given rise, once again, to the essence of politics, that is the founding proclamation of an exceptionality beyond all measure.

Indeed, to present this book's overall argument in a nutshell: The Caliphate is a form of radical hostility because it neither plays the conventional games of political forms, nor the formal game of war, nor the game of human rights.[37] It acts outside of forms. It rejects the global codes that have governed or framed politics as we have practiced it for the last fifty years. In its definition of the human (the relationship to humanity), in its profession of political faith (the nature of the state), in its recruitment of civilians and military personnel (the nature of societal organization), and in its battle strategy (the object and the method of an aggressive defensiveness), the Caliphate has introduced a radical distance between "us" and it. This distance is a response to the radical wrongdoings it sees inflicted by its enemies against Islam.

In all things, therefore, the Caliphate declares what is called in political philosophy a "differend":[38] The Caliphate has no dispute with those it calls "Crusaders" or with the "apostate" Muslim states, a dispute that could be resolved or managed at a negotiation table (as in the case of Iran) or through the coded game of armed relations (as in the case of North Korea). But the Caliphate having asserted the immeasurable wrongs inflicted on Islam by "us," proclaims something radically different from a dispute: It proclaims a "differend." In short: The war waged on Western democracies is without measure. And this is our immeasurable challenge.

Hence the Caliphate rejects all means and methods by which we measure confrontational policy and conflict resolution: It rejects our language (as a measure of things) and our political codes (as a common idiom) that allow the resolution of conflicts or the management of disputes. It rejects the possibility of a common language in politics whose codes, roles, procedures, and forums we would have defined, indeed have defined for two centuries. A politics to which even Communist regimes conformed and by which, in varying degrees, certain states, although recalcitrant or even rogue, nonetheless abide.

The Caliphate is beyond measure in politics. Therein lies its exceptional character: in asserting the differend and activating it.

Our effort ought to be in bringing the Caliphate, as a state, to see value, for themselves, in the way we make conflicts, however radical, fall within measures.

The Nine Angles for Approaching Jihadism

The components of the differend can be broken down into nine rhetorical units—rhetorical in the exact meaning of the word: devices and procedures made to produce persuasive effects, to wit:

— codes of political reasoning that break with a norm of rationality;
— an oratorical leadership whose charisma is inspired without being personal;

— a territory of action that is expandable at will as it is defined by holy recitation that generates a feeling of control over Space;

— a capacity as a strong language to parasitize diminished languages and to imitate them in order (not) to define key terms;

— a communications strategy that operates by diversion, accompanied with the use of a range of oratorical means, which functions as appeal and as transcendence;

— a strong link between the aesthetic and the ethical;

— a resetting of gender codes, as seen both by the positioning of women and by the reaffirmation of war as an embodiment of virility;

— its framing of actions by rites, sacrificial or not, that procure a feeling of control over Time, to which "we" respond with rhetorical codes that are themselves enfeebled, given the controls that burden our discourse community without burdening that of caliphal jihadism;

— the constitution of a volunteer and combatant population of a new and perilous kind, an event that propels "us" toward a foundational situation in politics, namely survival.

These nine elements were put into action in startling manner in the attack against Paris on November 13, 2015, and the ensuing communications assault. It is a comprehensive lesson in strategy that will be reproduced elsewhere. In strategy, this is called "a textbook case," a case, that is, that will be reproduced elsewhere, in another guerrilla attack of the same magnitude and sustained by the same kinetic propaganda processes. It will have to be in a capital city.

Paris, November 13, 2015:
A Comprehensive Lesson in Strategy

The November 13 attacks against the Parisian population offer a brutal synthesis of the rhetorical mechanisms that arm the Caliphate's new and radical war. At one time, the rivalry between the colonial powers for control in central Asia that gave rise to the birth of Afghanistan, the bastion of jihadism, was known as the Great Game. Henceforth the Great Game is being played against us, on our territory.

The Methodology of the Caliphate

Every game, no matter how brutal, has rules, and it is clear that the rulebook to this radical war is in the hands of the Caliphate. After a half-century in which the world had to play by our rules, a different set of rules for waging war has been imposed on us, on the ground, in propaganda, and even in our hearts. What are the rules of the game? The Caliphate's strategists call it a methodology. This methodology is military, but it is also intellectual and spiritual.

This term, *methodology*, appears out of place for designating a war in the Middle East and partisan guerrillas inside our borders, but let us recall Descartes and his *Discourse on Method:* A method is a "path" (*hodos* in ancient Greek, the path) and a discourse on method, or a methodology, the same expression and the same idea, denotes how by thinking correctly progress can be achieved directly toward a goal. The caliphal methodology is simply the Islamic discourse on method, fine-tuned by the Caliphate's think tank. It is a strategic plan. It is the Islamic equivalent of Clausewitz's *On War.*

It is also the road map where the commandos march, a route that starts in Mosul where the Caliph preaches; crosses ancient Ottoman Rumelia, Turkish-occupied slice of Europe; the Balkans, where provisions and ammunitions are hidden;[1] moves freely along the soft belly of Europe; and penetrates France. The at-all-costs offensive, analyzed earlier in connection with the theater of war, is equally applicable to the Caliphate's urban guerrilla tactics.

He who defines the rules of the game and holds the trump cards wins the game. The Caliphate's trump card is its method, inflexible in its objectives, plastic in its tactics, multipolar in its points of application, hypermodern on the terrain of influence that has become a true "public diplomacy," and served by spiritual leadership whose power we are no longer willing to admit in the West, not since the demise of the great ideologies.

We can, we must examine how caliphal propaganda methodically put in place a strategy of explanation and commentary regarding the November 13 attack so as to assess its arsenal of words in action.

We need to examine closely the programming of the second phase of the November 13 attack, that is, the mediatized assault. In methodology, everything fits together: the ground attack, the Internet attack. It is a grave mistake to believe that caliphal propaganda is a supplement: It is an organic element of each military operation. The assault must be followed by an assault of words and images in order to complete the military operation by a two-pronged propaganda operation, meaning both propagation (in the direction of Muslims) and provocative montage (in the direction of its enemies).

Media Offensive 1: The Victory Press Release

In the first instance, on November 14, an unofficial victory press release, in Arabic[2] and in French. Whoever composed it (not the narrator on the Internet, just a presenter)[3] was applying methodology.

The press release has two faces: the surface content and the hidden content. On the manifest side, it declares that the "soldiers of the Caliphate" have "taken as their target the capital of abomination and of perversion," to "sow fear in the hearts of the crusaders." The text opens, this is its apparent framework, with a citation from Sura 59 of the Koran, and closes by citing Sura 63. Between the two cited suras, the press release is grandiloquent, it accumulates every caliphal cliché that the speechwriter in charge of the French bureau knows we want to read—a hyperbolic "oriental" language, such as was explained at the start of this book. This is what the Caliphate knows we expect: We are being sent back a mirror image of what we wish to hear from the Caliphate.

But it is the press release's structure that permits access to its true dimension: Jihadist readers, or simply Muslims, are asked to understand that there is a spiritual path to be taken, an interpretative method.

You must therefore open the Koran to follow this path. Sura 59 is clear, it is dedicated to a tribe that refuses the message of God and that shuts itself away, vainly, in a fortress. If one knows God, it is futile to immure oneself in a fortress to deny his power. The immediate sense is that in Paris, it is as if we are in a fortress, a fortress that in fact is defenseless against the power of faith—whence the attacks. The framework has been established.

Sura 60 is devoted to the frequentation of women. There are, in fact, according to the Koran two ways of avoiding apostasy: abstaining from friendships with miscreants but most of all with their women, who can bring the temptations of impiety into a home. No relationships of proximity. Therefore, for anyone that can read, in this category fall all meeting places, all the trappings of sociability offered by the world of the infidels, a "bataclan" of human relations in effect (*bataclan* is both the name of the concert hall where the main massacre took place and a word equivalent to English *caboodle, hotchpotch*). Sura 61 promptly unleashes the "order to battle" evoking the figures of Moses, Jesus, Muhammad. Why? Each time God has spoken in this world, those that have received his word, the sura indicates, have turned a deaf ear to the revelation that followed: the Jews to the words of Jesus, Christians to the teaching of Muhammad. The people of God are divided where they should be in line, unanimous, prepared to fight Satan, and it is therefore against Jews and Christians that the true believers, Mohammedans, are lining up to prepare for battle. Sura 60 therefore targets forms of social proximity and Sura 61 forms of religious proximity. Sura 62, "Assembly of Believers," follows logically; it is devoted to the assembly for Friday prayers, to the homily, and to the manner in which it is appropriate to listen together, "prepared for battle," to commentaries on the word of God. Indeed, the attack against Paris took place on a Friday; the commandos had therefore listened to a sermon and then, before the attack, implored God with evening prayers, which the media failed to mention.

Next in our read-along, Sura 63, focusing on "hypocrites," that is, those who pretend to be Muslims, who follow in word but not in thought. Those who pretend to assemble on Fridays for prayers but who go to watch soccer games at night or drink beer on the terraces of cafés and listen to profligate music at the

Bataclan. Suras 59–63 are also cited, rigorously framing the victory press release: The first designates the infidels, the last the false Muslims. They conceal the intermediary suras, methodical applications of the Koran.

We are forced to admire the work of the speechwriter of the French bureau of Al-Hayat Media Center. We have here, as though further proof were needed, high-level expertise with an understanding of the lessons of rhetoric: Identify your audiences and act in such a way that a message can be polyvalent, target multiple audiences at once.

But the method does not end there. Intransigently, it follows its path.

Media Offensive 2: Phases of Propaganda

On November 20, a week after the attack, the Caliphate put out a new issue of its English publication, *Dābiq*.[4] Ignoring the press release, *Dābiq* provided, however, an inventory of recent "military operations." The assault against Paris was cited as one of a dozen other actions in the provinces (*wilayats*) of the Caliphate, from Bengal . . . to France. What for us is an unprecedented attack, a "horror," is to caliphal strategists a simple military action, a methodical movement of a piece on a chessboard the size of the Hexagon (as France is sometimes called), an act demonstrating a method of warfare, one element in their Great Game. France becomes one component of the nomenclature of zones in which the Caliphate has gained a foothold: France, as we know it, is already a caliphal territory—which as we saw in chapter 2 is precisely the strategy of the guerrillas for seizing territory, since caliphal partisans hold that they are forming a "global resistance" against a miscreant occupation that is "terrorizing" them by imposing its impious laws[5] on them, and against the war waged by the West in the Middle East, which they present as a "transgression."

France is treated as a *wilayat*, a province waiting to be governed by the Caliphate, with its population-in-waiting, those lost to apostasy as is the case of the Muslim soccer fans or those who have strayed into miscreant secular humanism, needing to be returned to the fold, placed back on the path of righteousness, by the "evidence" of a massacre—a sacrificial massacre, as we read above (chapter 9), must compel them to accept the evidence of conversion.

France has therefore duplicated itself: It exists as the land we know, with its rivers and mountains, its steeples and its fairground merry-go-rounds, its schools and its vineyards. Surreptitiously, a lining has slid underneath it, the *wilayat Fransa*, this territory hallucinated by the partisans of the Caliphate who are deployed there, but also by so-called "observant"[6] Muslims who, *ipso facto*, evolve in a parallel universe, propitious to favoring, among themselves, the ultimate conversion of a land where the "slumbering Muslim giant" is about to wake up.[7] So, in this shadow land another people begins to exist that duplicates and reduplicates the French people, a jihadist people whose populist resources have been described in chapter 12.

A rhetorical irony has gone unnoticed: Why did the Caliphate first publish its information in English and not in French? Because English is a global language, hence appropriate to a "global method of resistance," something French no longer is. The French public had to wait over two weeks before reading, in French, what the Caliphate thought about the assault. The Caliphate serves the French the same disdain that the French media pile on.

On November 21, the Caliphate's news machine posted a melodramatic video on the Internet, *Paris Has Fallen*.[8] It was released by its decentralized services in the *wilayat* of *Halab*[9] (Aleppo). It functions on three levels. By stating that it is dispatching this information from Aleppo, the Caliphate is showing that it is still operating from this province in Syria despite the battle raging there; it responds derisively to the French declared state of emergency; finally, it turns on its head a favorite explanation of supposed "self-radicalization," namely that some of those joining the Caliphate must be "vulnerable": "Your soldiers will come back to you mentally ill." This video had the desired effect—a frisson of scandal and horror, an emotional impact.

Not until November 30, more than two weeks after the assault but three days after the national tribute to its victims (November 27), did the Caliphate's public diplomacy at last deign to comment in French, in its magazine *Dār al-Islām*—it shifted from the emotional to the rational. In two movements.

In an initial maneuver, the original press release was revisited but, most of all, the Caliphate's Education Divan (council) held forth with a structured description of the profound causes of the attack, namely that our secular education (a cause, touched on in chapter 7, concerning the emigration of women)[10] turns humans into idolaters instead of believers. Sweeping aside cultural relativism, which in the optics of the Muslim Brotherhood is a useful tool and an objective ally of the Islamic cause (as part of their "cultural strategy"), the Caliphate's intellectuals get to the heart of the matter.

France is the absolute ideological enemy, the homeland of the Enlightenment that, having expelled all religion from public discourse and justly intolerant of any intrusion of faith in the domain of the Republic, is therefore worse than miscreant: It is rationalist and humanist. The Caliphate offers three solutions: An immediate one to the "Muslims who do not accept that their children should be raised amid these sins" is that they join the land of Islam and undertake the *hegira* toward the Caliphate (by one of three territorial movements as described in chapter 2). The other solution is to murder public schoolteachers. The third is a military attack by partisans, but the document does not need to list it, as November 13 speaks for itself, and triggers this unbending and orchestrated sequence of propaganda documents, true "public diplomacy" of a new kind.

In a second maneuver, the Caliphate, having patiently awaited the national tribute on November 27 before making its comments, that is, before taking action by commentary, responded almost verbatim to the speech by the French president: To his declaration "Paris, a city that radiates by day and glows by night . . . but we have love," Al-Hayat, implacable in its method, replied:

> Those who love each other for Allah . . . are people who are loved by Allah with no familial bonds between them and this love is not based on economic interest. . . . Their faces and their bodies radiate heavenly light.[11]

Between the two written explanations, the one on November 20 targeting a global audience and the one on November 30 targeting a French or Francophone audience, the Caliphate's media service additionally interjected a video in a third European language —in German, on the "costs of the war," particularly its human costs.[12]

This global, methodical media campaign came to an end in early December with the publication of a clear and precise primer on the methods of media manipulation.[13]

The second, mediatized, propagandistic, informational assault had ended.

The overall assault of November 13 was over, and became part of the lore and motivational Story of the Caliphate, ahead of the opportunistic massacres of San Bernardino and Orlando.

In terms of strategic communications, however, the assault heralded a series of carefully argued vituperations against Western culture, Christian or secular, which, carried aloft by further attacks across the United States and Europe in 2016, culminated in a near-doctrinal document, "Why We Hate You & Why We Fight You."[14]

Published in the summer of 2016, the theologians and intellectuals of the Caliphate summarized in six points their rationale for targeting the West; as they put it, "there is indeed a rhyme to our terrorism, warfare, ruthlessness, and brutality."

The six points are worth quoting as they provide the first comprehensive and explicit summation of the motivational war waged by the Caliphate against the West. The text, also a brief for action, destined for some seven thousand partisans deployed across Europe who are either poised for action or engaged in an increasingly low-intensity form of guerrilla warfare, is a blueprint for jihad:

1. We hate you, first and foremost, because you are non-believers; you reject the oneness of Allah—whether you realize it or not.
2. We hate you because you are non-believers, liberal societies permit the very things that Allah has prohibited while banning many of the things He has permitted, a matter that doesn't concern you because you separate religion and state, thereby granting supreme authority to your whims and desires via the legislators you vote into power.
3. In the case of the atheist fringe, we hate you and wage war against you because you disbelieve the existence of your Lord and Creator. You witness the extraordinarily complex makeup of created beings . . . but insist that they all came about through randomness and that one should be faulted, mocked, and ostracized for recognizing that

the astonishing signs we witness day after day are the creation of the Wise, All-Knowing Creator and not the result of accidental occurrence.

4. We hate you for your crimes against Islam and wage war against you to punish you for your transgressions against our religion. So long as your subjects continue to mock our faith, insult the prophets of Allah—including Noah, Abraham, Moses, Jesus, and Muhammad—we will continue to retaliate, not with slogans and placards but with bullets and knives.

5. We hate you for your crimes against Muslims; your drones and fighter jets bomb, kill, and maim our people around the world, and your puppets in the usurped lands of the Muslims oppress, torture, and wage war against anyone who calls to the truth.

6. We hate you for invading our lands and fight you to repel you and drive you out. As long as there is an inch of territory left for us to reclaim, jihad will continue to be a personal obligation on every single Muslim.[15]

In sum, the Caliphate's strategic communicators built on a series of attacks, starting with what has been described earlier and culminating in the slaughter of a priest in France (July 2016) to enunciate the driving motives behind those acts of jihad warfare and to frame future actions. As explained earlier in this book, judicial and law enforcement agencies that look for explicit orders sent by the Caliphate to its partisans are misguided in applying common investigation procedures to uncommon acts. If anything, this brief, so clearly articulated by the Caliphate's central command, provides the reason, the basis, the order of battle for any action to come, should the Islamic State collapse. And yet, reading the entire text, one is again struck by its coldly elegant language, its deadly choice of words, its purist theological references, and its vituperative sophistication. This is a literary text, a masterpiece of lethal eloquence, words crafted into weapons.

The Power of Letters

Actually, why such sophistication in the mediatized attack? Surely not to influence the territories attacked. Surely to proselytize. And still more surely, to offer the Caliphate's troops in the oriental theater of operations, those dispersed across foreign territories as urban guerrillas, moral support, a political vision, an assurance that in the event the center is no longer holding, its methodology will retain its influence.

But there is still more, what brings us to the very heart of this power of ideological propaganda: the construction of a caliphal archive on a grand scale.

The texts and videos but also the mass of declarations on so-called "social" networks emanating from soldiers, partisans, sympathizers of the Caliphate have now been integrated to form a huge library. This library of jihad joins a long, religious, hagiographic time of Islam and the already quite lengthy and rich tradition of "God's Rule."[16] The Caliphate can disappear in its present form, its library will remain and will serve as inspiration, as lesson, as model. It will survive, and it will come back to haunt us.

Could we ever have imagined that the age of universal electronic communication would beget not only a form of war never before seen but more strikingly, that it would take shape on a profoundly literary model, through content, style, language, the complexity of its montages of citations and references? No ideology, no social movement, no global program since the arrival of the Internet has understood how to transform this "e-mechanics"[17] of the mass electronic means of communications into such a universal, polyvalent, multidirectional instrument of force and to do so with such resolve in judgment and tactical aplomb.[18]

To those who for the last ten years have been idiotically repeating that "books are dead," that virtual snapshots and narcissistic text messages are the new literacy and to those, guiltier still, who claimed that the "humanities" were dead, it would behoove them to consider that the Caliphate has resurrected a multilingual, multimedia propaganda, composed of texts and sustained arguments, as well as an intelligent and militant filmography, and that by treating the Internet as a tool and by not elevating it to an ideal and end in itself, it has succeeded in creating a peerless ideological library.

The cruel paradox is that nothing disappears from the Internet—Christians were able to burn the library of Alexandria to the ground and reduce the literary monuments of Greek literature and science to ashes, but no one will be able to erase the library of the Caliphate. The Internet has been repurposed and, like Frankenstein's monster, has been turned against its maker, us.

It is possible too, we hope, that the lesson of November 13 might have been to make us, at last, realize that nothing can replace the culture of letters, the civilization of elevated writing and oratory that is specific to Western civilization. The power of the caliphal library is that it is gradually gaining a foothold, book after book, battle after battle, and that it is settling in our territories devastated by the decline in intelligence, in populations that were once cultured, which sink a little further into comfortable and insolent ignorance every day, only to emerge after a carnage to express their rage and tears, bearing lighted candles. Pathos can never take the place of culture. Cemeteries are mute.

Western history is a rhetorical graveyard: Since Homer, the forces of persuasion and forms of conviction have confronted one another, supplementing the strength of weapons and delineating the mental territories of struggles for domination. Each great age has seen the fall of a rhetorical form and its replacement by another—a debate among equals in the Athenian mode yielded to the imperious eloquence of Rome; Rome in turn bowed before Christian predication; the *ancien régime* fell when the American Founding Fathers and the great orators of the French Revolution spoke from the tribune; the nineteenth century witnessed the replacement of political debate by the economic transaction, "the power of money"; that prompted the rise of populist regimes which, from Lenin to Mao, gambled on the eloquent power of leaders guiding voiceless people. And then this too vanished.

For a half-century, we thought that the West would forever be cradled by the sound of its own voice—a tempered, good-natured tone, subject to being raised at times, but fundamentally quiet and content. A voice dead to the stirring power of speech that had scored the rise of empires and their fall. For a half-century our entire universe of political representations had evacuated the revolutionary and cataclysmic potential of the vital, pressing, extreme rhetoric of ideals. We listened to ourselves talking. We murmured in our everyday life. We conversed about our tepid disagreements. There was nothing but dialogue, conversation, management, sensible procedures, and temperance. We even came to censor any speech deemed "offensive." Up to now we have been living routine lives or surviving dreadful events. From now on, it is a matter of rising above ourselves and not merely being thankful for staying alive in the face of terror.

For the veil that covered our temperate illusions has been torn from top to bottom: The partisan or jihadi soldier has bounded onto the world stage, armed with weapons and speeches, terrifying and eloquent; the caliph has ascended to the tribune, he whose persuasive power raises armies and assembles a new people; the youth run to them; women undertake the great journey; cultures are annihilated; an energetic propaganda, hypermodern in its means but most ancient in its content, has taken over our mental horizon and parasitized our language and our discourse. Are we going to be the last tombstone in this graveyard of rhetoric? History has caught her breath: She now has a stentorian voice, and her breath is burning.

What is to be done? Stop believing that the course of the world found in us its fermata. Seek in our history the means to rally. Arm ourselves rhetorically, together, on a scale comparable to the Caliphate, for the time will come when, even as we fight it, we will have to speak to the Caliphate or to its successor, not only by stymieing it on the ground with imposing yet uncertain force but also, and principally, by trying to counteract it on the terrain of persuasive ideas. The fall of Mosul will not extinguish the fire. Combatting ideas with ideas requires words. Weighted words. Persuasion. And the will to persuade. Do we possess the will? It is doubtful, so far. Because such a will implies that we take stock without prejudice of our own illusions, cease to be comfortable, and consider coolly that the doors are closing rapidly and irremediably on politics and peace by transaction and consent. We and our children have been pushed into a new world disorder where bellicose peace is likely to be the norm. The Caliphate has resurrected politics at its most fundamental energy: the brutally systematic creation of power, driven by eloquent transcendence and harnessing in the process human, too human, emotions. This new world is not for the faint-hearted. Nor for the soft-spoken.

Notes

PROLOGUE
The Caliphate's Rhetorical Power

1. Going forward, *Caliphate* shall designate the Islamic State, and *caliphal* shall be the adjective form.

2. Elliott Friedland, *The Islamic State: Report*, Clarion Project, Washington, D.C., May 10, 2015, available at www.clarionproject.org. This site archives the Caliphate's publications in English, past issues of *Dābiq* and current ones of *Rumiyah*.

3. *Dār al-Islām*, January 2, 2015, 2, available at www.archive.org. This quotation from Ecclesiastes 3:1–15 is doubly ironic: On the one hand, no French reader would ever pick up on it; the Caliphate's communication agency knew this full well and therefore is playing a game; on the other hand, it is a way of reminding French Catholics, who are few and far between, that Christian Scripture is simply a step toward the Quran, or the final revelation. I thank Jaya Aninda Chatterjee, assistant editor at Yale University Press, for pointing out the quotation.

4. Philippe-Joseph Salazar, *Mahomet: Récits français de la vie du Prophète* (Mohammed, French accounts of the life of the Prophet) (Paris: Klincksieck, 2005).

5. Arabic words are not transliterated according to strict philological rules.

6. Ibn Rajab Al-Hanbalî, *La Profession de foi* (The profession of faith) (Lyon: Tawhid, 2004).

7. Tom Holland, "We Must Not Deny the Religious Roots of Islamic State," *New Statesman*, March 17, 2015, available at www.newstatesman.com.

8. Jérôme Fourquet, "La douche: 65% des Français ne sont plus sensibles aux termes 'République' et 'valeurs républicaines,'" Ifop poll on the republican values and analysis by Vincent Tournier, *Atlantico*, May 10, 2015, available at www.atlantico.fr.

9. Abu Muhammad al-Julani, "Victory from God and Conquest Is Close," audio message, April 1, 2015, available at www.pietervanostaeyen.wordpress.com.

10. Grand Ayatollah Sayyid Ruhollah Mūsavi Khomeini, spiritual leader of the Islamic Republic of Iran from 1979 to 1989.

11. Ruhollah al-Musavi al-Khomeini, *Imam's Final Discourse*, Tehran, 1983.

12. *Peak of Eloquence, Nahjul Balagha*, Tahrike Tarsile Qur'an, 2009 (compilation of the words of Ali, at the source of Shi'ism).

13. The authoritative Arabic-French edition of Ali's speeches highlights a "path/ road of eloquence" and not a poetic "peak" (see previous note), that is the same conquering concept of a "method" or path of terror to which we will return in the epilogue. Ali Ibn Abi Talib, *La Voie de l'éloquence*, Beyrouth et Le Caire, Dar Al-Kitab Al-Lubnani et Dar Al-Kitab Al-Masri, 2nd ed., 1989.

14. *Dār al-Islām*, December 1, 2014, 2, available at www.archive.org.

15. Joseph Garcin de Tassy, "La rhétorique des nations musulmanes, d'après le traité persan intitulé *Hadâyik ul-balâgât* (The rhetoric of Muslim nations, based on the Persian treatise *Hadâyik ul-balâgât*)," *Journal asiatique*, November 1844, 366–408, available at www.gallica.bnf.fr. *Hadâyik ul-balâgât* was written by Shamsuddin Fakhir in the mid-eighteenth century in the Hindustani language.

16. Ibrahim Madkour, *L'Organon d'Aristote dans le monde arabe: ses traductions, son étude et ses applications. Analyse puisée principalement à un commentaire inédit d'Ibn Sînâ* (Aristotle's Organon in the Arab world: Its translations, its study, and its applications. Analysis focusing principally on an unpublished commentary by Ibn Sina) (Paris: Vrin, 1935).

17. Miguel Cruz Hernández, *Histoire de la pensée en terre d'islam* (A history of thought in the land of Islam) (Paris: Desjonquères, 2005).

18. Averroës, *Decisive Treatise and Epistle Dedicatory* (Provo, UT: Brigham Young University Press, 2002).

19. *An-Nawawi's Forty Hadith*, Islamic Texts Society, August 1, 1997.

20. Ibn Taymiyya, *Épître sur le sens de l'analogie (Epistle on the meaning of analogy)* (Beirut: Al-Bouraq, 1996). Late-13th-century, early-14th-century author often cited by the Caliphate; see *Dār al-Islām*, December 2014, 5.

21. Abu Hamid al-Ghazali, *Al-Ghazali on the Lawful and the Unlawful: Book XIV of the Revival of the Religious Sciences*, Ghazali Series, Islamic Texts Society, 2014, 1st edition.

22. Colin Bunzel, "32 Islamic State fatwas," March 2, 2015, available at www.jiha dica.com.

23. Averroës, *Decisive Treatise and Epistle Dedicatory*, § 20. Translation slightly modified by the author. Al-Ghazali, *Averroës and the Interpretation of the Qur'an* (Routledge, New York, 2010).

24. Al-Ghazali, *Averroës and the Interpretation of the Qur'an*, 178.

25. Abdel-Magid Turki, "Pour ou contre la légalité du séjour des musulmans en territoire reconquis par les chrétiens" (For or against the legality of Moslems staying in territory reconquered by Christians), May 20, 2000. "Territory reconquered by Christians" covers Spain, Sicily, Balkans, and the Caucasus.

26. *Dār al-Islām*, January 2, 2015, 6.

27. John Hall, "A Hug from the Executioner," *Mail Online*, April 23, 2015, available at www.dailymail.co.uk.

28. *An-Nawawi's Forty Hadith*, hadith 42.

29. Colin Bunzel and William McCants, "Experts Weigh In (part 1): How Does ISIS Approach the Islamic scripture?" Brookings Institution, March 24, 2015, available at www.brookings.edu.

30. Ahmed Bouyerdene, *L'Humanisme et l'Humanité en islam* (Humanism and humanity in Islam) (Paris: Fondation pour l'innovation politique, 2015); John Ware, "Inside the World of 'Non-Violent' Islamism," *Standpoint*, March 2015, available at www.standpointmag.co.uk.

ONE

The Caliph Speaks

1. Caliph Ibrahim will be referred to as Ibrahim or al-Baghdadi interchangeably.

2. Abu Bakr al-Baghdadi, *Khotba by the Emir of Believers*, sermon of proclamation of the Caliphate, video, July 5, 2014, available on the Ansa Al-Haqq site with a partial English translation at www.ansar-alhaqq.net and www.ansaaar1.word press.com and, from MEMRI TV, on YouTube with subtitles in English, available at www.youtube.com/watch?v=Ro9FmLnWC8E.

3. "Islamic State releases 'al-Baghdadi message,'" BBC, May 15, 2015.

4. Matt Bradley and Maria Abi Habib, "Video Purportedly Shows Islamic State Leader," *Wall Street Journal*, July 5, 2014, available at www.wsj.com.

5. Ramzy Baroud, "'Islamic State' Mystery: The Anti-History of a Historic Phenomenon," *Middle East Eye*, February 17, 2015, available at www.middle easteye.net.

6. Ali Hashem, "The Many Names of Abu Bakr al-Baghdadi," *Al-Monitor*, March 23, 2015, available at www.al-monitor.com.

7. U.S. Department of State, *Designations of Foreign Terrorist Fighters*, September 24, 2014, available at www.state.gov.

8. Philip Halldén, "What Is Arab Islamic Rhetoric? Rethinking the History of Muslim Oratory Art and Homiletics," *International Journal of Middle East Studies* 37 (2005): 19–38.

9. Zakaria Makri, *Le Tajwîd, règles de la lecture coranique* (Tajweed, the rules of koranic recitation) (Lyon: Tawhid, 2005).

10. The doctrine of the four idols, often used in rhetoric, comes from Francis Bacon, *Novum Organum*, Book 1 (Chicago: University of Chicago Press, 1952).

11. On the status of the states resulting from the breakup of Yugoslavia, see Andre Pellet, "The Opinions of the Badinter Arbitration Committee," *European Journal of International Law* 3, no. 1 (1992): 178–85, available at www.ejil.org. At the inception, the Montevideo Convention (1933) provided four criteria for the definition of a state.

12. Pellet, "Opinions," 182.

13. Bernard Lewis, *The Political Language of Islam* (Chicago: University of Chicago Press, 1988).

14. Patricia Crone, *God's Rule: Government and Islam* (New York: Columbia University Press, 2004).

15. Andrew F. March and Marie Revkin, "Caliphate of Law," *Foreign Affairs*, April 15, 2015, available at www.foreignaffairs.com.

16. In the speeches of William Pitt to the Communes under the Convention. Referred to in my introduction to "The Rhetorical Shape of International Conflicts," *Javnost–The Public* 12, no. 4 (2005).

17. Aaron Y. Zelin, *The Islamic State Model*, ICSR, London, January 29, 2015, available at www.icsr.info.

18. Henry Kissinger, *World Order* (New York: Penguin, 2014); see also the commentary by James Traub, "The Problem with Kissinger's *World Order*," *Foreign Policy*, May 5, 2015, available at www.foreignpolicy.com.

TWO

Naming the Territory of Terror

1. *French Penal Code*, legislative section L.IV, Title II: On terrorism, chapter 1: "On Acts of Terrorism," art. 421-1.

2. U.S. Code (/uscode/text) > Title 18 (/uscode/text/18) > Part I (/uscode/text/18/part-I) > Chapter 113B (/uscode/text/18/part-I/chapter-113B) > § 2331.

3. *Corpus Juris Civilis*, edited by Théodore Mommsen and Paul Krüger, *Digesta*, L, 16, *De verborum significatione*, §239 (Berlin: Weidmann, 1889).

4. U.S. Department of State, *Terrorist Designations of Groups Operating in Syria*, May 14, 2014, available at www.state.gov. U.S. Department of State, *Country Reports on Terrorism 2013*, "Foreign Terrorist Organizations," ch. 6, April 2014, available at www.state.gov.

5. See the updated report by Katherine Bauer, ed., *Beyond Syria and Iraq: Examining Islamic State Provinces* (Washington, D.C.: Washington Institute for Near East Policy, 2016).

6. Erin Marie Saltman and Charlie Winter, *Islamic State: The Changing Face of Modern Jihadism* (London: Quilliam, 2014), available at www.quilliamfoun dation.org.

7. Lenin, *What Is To Be Done?* (1902), available at www.marxists.org.

8. Patricia Crone, "'Jihad': Idea and History," *Cosmopolis* 1 (2015): 83–88; Osama Bin Laden, *Messages to the World* (New York: Verso, 2005).

9. John M. Owen IV, "From Calvin to the Caliphate," *Foreign Affairs*, May–June 2015, available at www.foreignaffairs.com. Bruce Lawrence, ed., *Messages to the World: The Statements of Osama Bin Laden* (New York: Verso, 2005).

10. Bernard Lewis, *From Babel to Dragomans: Interpreting the Middle East* (New York: Oxford University Press, 2004).

11. *How to Survive in the West: A Mujahid Guide*, terrorist guide, 2015. E-book available at www.memrijttm.org/e-book-distributed-via-twitter-how-to-sur vive-in-the-west-a-mujahid-guide.html.

12. In theory: "Hijrah Inevitably Ends with Forgiveness," *Rumiyah*, 4, December 7, 2016, 3. In practice: *Hijrah to the Islamic State: What to Pack Up, Who to Contact, Where to Go*, 2015, available at www.usarchive.org. Anonymous, "Escape to the Islamic State," November 27, 2014, available at www.news.vice.com (eleven pages of commentary furnish a compendium of clichés that reflect poorly on the Western public's understanding of jihadism).

13. *Profiles of Perpetrators of Terrorism—United States (PPT-US)*, START, U.S. Department of Homeland Security and University of Maryland, June 30, 2012, available at www.start.umd.edu; "UN Says '25,000 Foreign Fighters' Joined Islamist Militants," BBC, April 2, 2015, available at www.bbc.com; see also the updated report by Brian Dodwell, Daniel Milton, and Don Rassler, *Then and Now: Comparing the Flow of Foreign Fighters to AQI and the Islamic State*, "Combating Terrorism Center at West Point" conference, West Point, New York, December 2016, available at www.ctc.usma.edu.

14. Bilal Philips, *Salvation through Repentance* (Lyon, Tawhid, 1999), available at www .bilalphilips.com/wpcontent/uploads/2013/07/Salvation%20Through%20 Repentance.pdf.

15. *Dār al-Islām*, January 2, 2015, 2.

16. Torgier P. Krokfjord, "Voldssiralen har eskalert," *Dagbladet*, April 23, 2015, available at www.dagbladet.no.

17. The June 2015 "Boston plot" to behead controversial political commentator Pamela Geller.

18. Soren Seelow, "Le suspect de l'attentat déjoué n'avait pas le profil d'un délinquant radicalisé" (The profile of the suspect in the recent attack is not

that of a radicalized criminal), *Le Monde*, April 23, 2015, available at www
.lemonde.fr; Aiz Zemouri, "Djihad: qui sont les hommes interpellés à Lunel?"
(Jihad: Who are the men summoned to Lunel?), *Le Point*, April 25, 2015,
available at www.lepoint.fr; Josepha Bougnon, "De Maxime Hauchard à
Abou Abdallah Al-Faransi, itinéraire d'un Français parti faire le Djihad"
(From Maxime Hauchard to Abou Abdallah Al-Faransi, the itinerary of a
Frenchman leaving to undertake Jihad), *Jerusalem Post*, November 27, 2014,
available at www.jpost.com; "Le cyber-djihadiste français al-Normandy condamné à un an de prison ferme" (The French cyberjihadist al-Normandy
condemned to one year of prison without parole), France 24, March 4,
2014, available at www.france24.com. An American example of a college-
educated terrorist is Ohio State University jihadist Abdul Razak Ali Artan,
as reported by Robin Wright, "The Hand of ISIS at Ohio State," November
29, 2016, *The New Yorker*, available at www.newyorker.com/news/news-desk/
the-hand-of-isis-at-ohio-state.

19. James Dowling, Angus Thompson, and Tom Ninear, "Jake Bilardi Wrote of
Terror and Death in His Online Blog," *Herald Sun*, March 12, 2015, available
at www.heraldsun.com.au.

20. "Salafists Want to Establish Their Own Islamic State in Germany," Ahlul-
Bayt News Agency-ABNA-ShiaNews, April 23, 2015, available at www.abna
24.com; Daniel Heinke and Jan Raudszus, "German Foreign Fighters in Syria
and Iraq," ICSR, January 22, 2015, available at www.iscr.info; Pieter Van
Ostaeyen, "Belgium's Syria Fighters: A Statistical Analysis," February 19–
March 21, 2014, available at https://pietervanostaeyen.wordpress.com.

21. Isabelle Grangaud and Nicolas Michel, introduction to the issue on "Identity," *Revue des mondes musulmans et de la Méditerranée* 127 (2010): 13–27.

22. Scott Shane, "From Minneapolis to ISIS: An American's Path to Jihad," *New
York Times*, March 21, 2015, available at www.nytimes.com; Joanna Par-
aszczuk, "IS Threatens to 'Burn America' in New Propaganda Video," Radio
Free Europe, April 13, 2015, available at www.rferl.org.

23. "Who Are Australia's Radicalized Muslims?" BBC, March 12, 2015, available at www.bbc.com; Joanna Paraszczuk, "Australian IS Militant Calls for
Attacks on Civilians," Radio Free Europe, April 22, 2015, available at www
.rferl.org.

24. Christopher Anzalone, "Canadian Foreign Fighters in Iraq and Syria," *CTC
Sentinel*, April 30, 2015, available at www.ctc.usma.edu; Islamic Social Services Association, *United against Terrorism*, National Council of Canadian Muslims, Royal Canadian Mounted Police, 2014, available at www.issaservices
.com.

25. Sami A. Aldeeb Abu-Sahlieh, *La Fatiha et la Culture de la haine. Interprétation
du 7ᵉ verset à travers les siècles* (The Fatiha and the culture of hatred: Interpretation of the 7th verse through the centuries), Centre de droit arabe et

musulman, 2014. An accurate study based on exegeses by Moslem theologians from the different schools of Islamic law.

26. This video of April 19, 2015, combines a good course in the political history of the variants of Christianity and witness accounts and a double mass execution of Christians, before ending on an exhortation to those that have "strayed" (namely Armenian and Syrian Christians). The video title is thus a terse abbreviation of a statement that should read in full: Christians will be punished until there comes to them clear evidence that Islam fulfills the message of Jesus Christ. "Islamic State *New Release:* 'Until There Came to Them Clear Evidence,'" *Sharia Unveiled,* available at https://shariaunveiled .wordpress.com/2015/04/19/islamic-state-new-release-until-there-came -to-them-clear-evidence-uncut-video.

27. Orlando Crowcroft, "Why Are So Many Young British Muslims Joining Islamic State in Iraq and Syria?" *International Business Times,* April 9, 2015, available at www.ibtimes.co.uk. Brenda Stoter, "Radicalized Western Women Lead Children into Islamic State," *Al-Monitor,* April 13, 2015, available at www.al-monitor.com.

THREE

"Terrorism," Linguistic Subversion

1. Leon Trotsky, *Terrorism and Communism* (1920), available at www.marxists.org.
2. Jean-Paul Sartre, *Critique of Dialectical Reason* (London: New Left Books, 1976). Numerous pages are devoted to the practice of Terror, in both the first and the second volumes—a unique philosophical meditation on terror as a practice of social and transformational solidarity or, as Sartre calls it, a "Fraternity-Terror."
3. See the conversation on Twitter with the hashtag #IS (sampling examined, April 20–27, 2015).
4. "ISIS hat eine multi-ethnische Armee kreiert; nahezu eine Fremdenlegion, um deren Territorium zu sichern" (ISIS has created a multi-ethnic army; almost a Foreign Legion to secure their territory), *Dābiq* (German edition), July 1, 2014, 33.
5. *Dābiq,* April 8, 2015, 17.
6. France 24, English-language channel.
7. Paul Bacot, Dominique Desmarchelier, and Jean-Paul Honoré, "Les usages politiques d'une réduction" (The political uses of a reduction), *Mots. Les langages du politique* 95 (2011): 5–10.
8. Office of the United Nations High Commissioner for Human Rights, *Report . . . on the human rights situation in Iraq in the light of abuses committed by the so-called Islamic State in Iraq and the Levant and associated groups,* Advance un-

edited version, March 13, 2015. The BBC refuses to use the term *Daesh* on the grounds that it is "pejorative."

9. Adam Taylor, "France Is Ditching the 'Islamic State' Name—and Replacing It with a Label the Group Hates," *Washington Post*, September 17, 2014, available at www.washingtonpost.com.

10. "Islamic Cult a Death Cult—Abbott," *IOL News*, September 1, 2014, available at www.iol.co.za. Cited by François Hollande, November 27, 2015.

11. Pieter Van Ostaeyen, "On the Origin of the 'Name' DAESH—The Islamic State in Iraq and as-Shām," February 18, 2014, available at https://pieterva nostaeyen.wordpress.com.

12. Mark Sedgwick, "Jihadism, Narrow and Wide: The Dangers of Loose Use of an Important Term," *Perspectives on Terrorism* 9, no. 2 (2015): 34–41.

13. "The return of the Kilafah," *Dābiq*, July 1, 2014; "Die Rückkehr der Khilafah" (German version), July 2014.

14. A crucial concept developed by Jean-Pierre Faye, *Langages totalitaires* (Totalitarian languages) (Paris: Hermann, 1972).

15. Fred M. Donner, "Qur'ânicization of religio-political discourse in the Umayyad period" *Revue des mondes musulmans et Méditerranée* 129 (July 2011): 79–92, available at http://remm.revues.org/7085. On the "Koranic taboo," see the late Abdelwahab Meddeb, *Sortir de la malédiction. L'islam entre civilisation et barbarie* (Exiting the malediction: Islam between civilization and barbarism) (Paris: Le Seuil, 2008).

16. Tariq Ramadan and Yûsuf Al-Qardâwî (dir.), *Recueil de fatwas. Avis juridiques concernant les musulmans d'Europe* (Compilation of fatwas: Legal opinions concerning Europe's Muslims) (Lyon: Tawhid, 2002).

17. "Un Haut-Normand à l'État islamique: Le témoignage d'une habitante de son village" (A man from Upper Normandy in the Islamic State: An account by a resident of his village), Tendance Ouest (radio station), November 17, 2014, available at www.tendanceouest.com.

18. In the 7th issue of *Dābiq*, there was an interview with Coulibaly's wife "that in his loyalty toward the Caliphate, he had had the wisdom to place in safety here while preparing her conversion and his attack, may he be blessed" (p. 50). In short, a premeditated treason.

19. French military code, *Code de justice militaire*, art. L331–L332: "Le fait, en temps de guerre, par tout Français ou tout militaire au service de la France, de porter les armes contre la France constitue un acte de trahison puni de la réclusion criminelle à perpétuité et de 750,000 euros d'amende." (French Military Justice Code, art. L331–L332: "The act in times of war, by any French person, or any member of the military in the service of France, of taking up arms against France, constitutes an act of treason punishable by life in prison and by a 750,000 euros fine.")

20. French Penal Code, Treason and Espionage, article 411: "Intelligence with

a foreign power, a foreign undertaking or organization or an enterprise or organization under foreign control, or their agents, with a view to fomenting hostilities or acts of aggression against France, is punished by thirty years' criminal detention and a fine of €450,000. The same penalties apply to furnishing a foreign power, a foreign undertaking or organization, or an undertaking or organization under foreign control, or their agents, with the means to start hostilities or commit acts of aggression against France."

21. 18 U.S.C. § 2381: U.S. Code - Section 2381: Treason: "Whoever, owing allegiance to the United States, levies war against them or adheres to their enemies, giving them aid and comfort within the United States or elsewhere, is guilty of treason and shall suffer death, or shall be imprisoned not less than five years and fined under this title but not less than $10,000; and shall be incapable of holding any office under the United States," available at http://codes.lp.findlaw.com/uscode/18/I/115/2381.

22. A circular from the French Republic's minister of the interior to heads of police, domestic security agencies, foreigners in France agency, prefects (regional administrators), etc.: *Lutte contre le terrorisme* (Fight against terrorism), February 19, 2015. Law no. 2014-1353 of November 13, 2014, reinforcing the measures relative to the fight against terrorism, *Journal Officiel* no. 0263, November 14, 2014, available at www.legifrance.gouv.fr.

23. In Canada, despite draconian new security laws, agencies have some difficulty in identifying and naming acts of treason. Nick Logan, "The Trouble with Charging Canadian ISIS Fighters," *Global News*, December 12, 2014, available at www.oped.news.

24. The French Republic, National Assembly, *Rapport d'information déposé . . . par la commission des lois constitutionnelles . . . sur l'indignité nationale . . . par M. Jean-Jacques Urvoas* (Information report filed . . . by the standing committee on constitutional laws . . . on national indignity), March 25, 2015, 22.

FOUR
Digital Caliphate

1. Imad Sitiou, "Morocco battles Islamic State cells," *Al-Monitor*, May 6, 2015, available at www.al-monitor.com.

2. Citation from Islamic Organization for Education, the Sciences and Culture (ISESCO), *Strategy of Islamic Cultural Action in the West* (Rabat: ISESCO, 2001), 70. This report supposedly came from a moderate organization. Adrian Shtumi, "Ethnic Albanians Foreign Fighters in Iraq and Syria," *CTC Sentinel* 8, no. 4, April 30, 2015, available at www.cts.usma.edu; Anonymous, "Background of Terrorist Attacks in FYROM (Macedonia)," available at www.liveleak.com, based on Vladimir Dukanvic, "Канвас и учк на делу у македонији," May 10, 2015, available at www.standard.rs; Joanna Par-

aszczuk, "Report Finds Alarming Outflow of Kosovars to Islamic State," Radio Free Europe, April 15, 2015, available at www.rferl.org.

3. "Islamic State Fighters Claim to Be on Streets of Rome," The Clarion Project, April 29, 2015, available at www.clarionproject.org; Mahmoud Kilani, "Parquet de Milan: Le suspect était en Italie lors de l'attentat de Tunis" (Milan prosecutor: The suspect was in Italy at the time of the Tunis attack), *Anadolu Agency*, May 21, 2015, available at www.aa.com.tr. Abdel Majid Touil had embarked with migrants.

4. "ISIS Evades Russian Bans to Spread Propaganda on Social Media," World News Radio, January 19, 2015, available at www.tunin.com; Joanna Paraszczuk, "Radicalized in Moscow, Killed in Syria: The Story of an IS Sniper," Radio Free Europe, April 30, 2015; "Who's Recruiting Young Men from Georgia to Fight in Syria?" Radio Free Europe, April 13, 2015, available at www.rferl.org.

5. "Hyderabad: 14 Students Planning to Join Islamic State Stopped at Airport," Zee Media Bureau, May 6, 2015, available at www.zeenews.india.com.

6. James Brandon, "Indonesian Arrests Underline Influence of Islamic State," *Terrorism Monitor* 13, no. 4 (April 2015): 2–3, available at www.jamestown.org; "Singapore Detains Two 'Self-Radicalized' Teens, One Aimed to Join Islamic State," Reuters, May 27, 2015, available at www.reuters.com.

7. Map of the Caliphate, *Alrakoba*, March 12, 2015, available at www.alrakoba.net. See also Djordje Djukic and Evan Centanni, "War in Iraq: Map of Islamic State control in May 2015," *Political Geography Now*, May 22, 2015, available at www.polgeonow.com (updated regularly).

8. David Vergun, "More Ground Robots to Serve alongside Soldiers Soon." The Official Homepage of the United States Army, April 8, 2015, available at www.army.mil.

9. Caliphate material is relatively available at www.clarionproject.org, www.jihadology.net, www.archive.org, and www.postedeveille.ca.

10. Gabriel Weimann, *New Terrorism and New Media*, Wilson Center, 2014, available at www.wilsoncenter.org; Cristina Archetti, "Terrorism, Communication, and the New Media: Explaining Radicalization in the Digital Age," *Perspectives on Terrorism* 9, no. 1 (2015): 49–59.

11. Daniel Pipes, president of Middle East Forum, "ISIS Attacks on the West: The Terror Group's Impact Is More Inspirational Than 'Organizational,'" *Washington Times*, May 21, 2015, available at www.washingtontimes.com.

12. The Caliphate's media center, Al-Hayat, has been managed by German-Ghanaian ex-rapper Denis Cuspert and, as "editor-in-chief," by the Syrian French-born U.S. citizen Ahmad Abousamra, which may account for the fluency of publications in German and French. Soeren Kern, "Germany's 'Demagogue of Armed Jihad,'" Gatestone Institute, May 26, 2015, www.gatestoneinstitute.org. Thomas Joscelyn, "How a US Citizen Became a Key

Player in the Islamic State's Rivalry with al Qaeda," *FDD's Long War Journal*, April 7, 2017, www.longwarjournal.org. U.S. Department of State, *Terrorist Designation of Denis Cuspert*, February 9, 2015, available at www.state.gov.

13. "Stop-Djihadisme," an official video from the French government; available at www.stop-djihadisme.gouv.fr. The site also offers a brochure of nine pictograms to assist in detecting "signs" of radicalization, for example, someone no longer eating "the French way" (the pictogram depicts a crossed-out baguette).

14. An English study, pre-Caliphate, enumerates a list of voluntarist actions that are signs of self-recruitment. Mehmood Naqshbandi, *Problems and Practical Solutions to Tackle Extremism; and Muslim Youth and Community Issues*, Shrivenham Papers, 1, Shrivenham, Defence Academy of the United Kingdom, 2006, available at www.defenceacademy.mod.uk.

15. Dominic Casciani, "Islamic State: Profile of Mohammed Emwazi aka 'Jihadi John,'" BBC, March 8, 2015, www.bbc.com.

16. Ashleen McGhee, "Islamic State: Australian-Trained Doctor Tareq Kamleh Appears in IS Propaganda Video Urging Jihad in Syria," ABC, April 26, 2015, available at www.abc.net.au.

17. The U.S. Center for Strategic Counterterrorism Communications (CSCC) made the same mistake, and it backfired the same way: *Welcome to ISIS Land*. Greg Miller and Scott Higham, "In a Propaganda War against ISIS, the U.S. Tried to Play by the Enemy's Rules," *Washington Post*, May 8, 2015, available at www.washingtonpost.com.

18. McGhee, "Islamic State."

19. Dominique Casciani, "Woolwich: How Did Michael Adebolajo Become a Killer?" BBC, December 19, 2013, available at www.bbc.com.

20. For example, *From the Battlefields of Syria*, available at chechclear.tumbler.com.

21. Jake Bilardi, "From Melbourne to Ramadi: My Journey," January 13, 2015, is blocked on Google (https://fromtheeyesofamuhajir.wordpress.com/2015/01/13/from-melbourne-to-ramadi-my-journey/+&cd=2&hl=en&ct=clnk&gl=au), but extracts can be read in "Jake Bilardi: Blog Believed to Belong to Australian Teenager Details Journey behind Radicalization," ABC, March 12, 2015, available at www.abc.net.au; see also Elize Potaka, interview with Jake Bilardi, *SBS News*, March 12, 2015 (conducted on Twitter in December 2014), available at www.sbs.com.au.

22. Amarnath Amaringsham, "Elton 'Ibrahim' Simpson's Path to Jihad in Garland, Texas," *War on the Rocks*, May 14, 2015, available at www.warontherocks.com.

23. "US Military Drops Graphic Leaflets near Syrian City to Deter Possible Islamic State Recruits," Associated Press, March 26, 2015, available at www.foxnews.com.

24. Max Weber, *The Vocation Lectures* (Indianapolis: Hackett, 2004).

25. Gabriel Weimann, *New Terrorism and New Media* (Washington, D.C.: Wilson Center, 2014), available at www.wilsoncenter.org; the quantitative and detailed study contradicting it is J. M. Berger and Jonathan Morgan, *The ISIS Twitter Census* (Washington, D.C.: Brookings Institution, 2015), available at www.brookings.edu. The Caliphate source account has been shut down: https://twitter.com/Muhammad_masry4.

26. Jytte Klausen, "Tweeting the Jihad: Social Media Networks of Western Foreign Fighters in Syria and Iraq," *Studies in Conflict and Terrorism* 38, no. 1 (2015): 1–22. Damien Leloup, "Paris, Bruxelles, Toulouse . . . la radicalisation des terroristes n'a pas eu lieu sur le Web" (Paris, Brussels, Toulouse . . . the radicalization of terrorists did not take place on the web), *Le Monde*, January 12, 2015, available at www.lemonde.fr; Damien Leloup, "Djihadisme sur le Web: les exagérations de Bernard Cazeneuve" (Jihadism on the Web: The exaggerations of Bernard Cazeneuve) (then minister of the interior), *Le Monde*, February 20, 2015, available at www.lemonde.fr. See, for example, S. A. Tatham, *Strategic Communication*, Shrivenham, Defence Academy of the United Kingdom, 2008. There is little information for the moment on the schemas of implementation in France: Laurent Lagneau, "Une unité militaire française chargée de contrer la propagande djihadiste sur Internet" (A French military unit in charge of countering jihadist propaganda on the Internet), *Zone militaire*, April 25, 2015, available at www.opex360.com. On the other hand: Kyle Matthews, "Five Ways to Fight ISIS Online," *Conseil international du Canada/Open Canada*, February 14, 2015, available at www.opencanada.org; Peter D. Neumann and Tim Stevens, *Countering Online Radicalization: A Strategy for Action* (London: ICSR, 2009), available at www.icsr.info.

FIVE

Strongspeak vs. Weakspeak

1. Herodotus, *History* (Chicago: University of Chicago Press, 1952), 1:135.

2. Luciano Canfora, *Thucydide. Le Dialogue des Méliens et des Athéniens* (Paris: Éditions de l'éclat, 2013); *The Melian Dialogue*, trans. Rex Warner, available at http://lygdamus.com/resources/New%20PDFS/Melian.pdf.

3. Philippe-Joseph Salazar, "Strategic Communications: A New Field for Rhetoric," *Tribune libre*, no. 33, Centre français de recherche sur le renseignement, September 6, 2013, available at www.cf2r.org.

4. Philippe-Joseph Salazar, *Amnistier l'apartheid* (Granting amnesty to apartheid) (Paris: Seuil, 2004).

5. In September 2014, more than twelve thousand foreign fighters representing eighty-one countries—of which three thousand were European—responded to the appeal. Jeanine de Roy van Zuijdewijn, "The Foreign Fighters' Threat." *Perspectives on terrorism* 8, no. 5 (2014): 59–73. Anonymous, "Les

'*Foreign Fighters*' étudiés" (The "Foreign Fighters" studied), *TTU-Lettre heb-domadaire d'informations stratégiques*, no. 972, April 8, 2015, 1, 6. In April 2015 the numbers grew to twenty thousand, of which six thousand were Europeans. *TTU-Lettre hebdomadaire d'informations stratégiques*, no. 973, April 15, 2015, 2. In other words, the group doubled in six months. See a report from late 2016 by Dominic Evans and Ahmed Rasheed: "'Crashing Waves' of Jihadists Fray Soldiers' Nerves in Mosul Battle," Reuters, November 10, 2016, available at www.reuters.com.

6. Ronald H. Carpenter, *Rhetoric in Martial Deliberations and Decision Making* (Columbia: University of South Carolina Press, 2004).

7. This ascension is different from the Christian notion: In Islamic lore, Jesus, or Isa, was not crucified and shall return in the time of the final battle against Satan as commander-in-chief of the Muslim armies.

8. "Légers ou lourds, lancez-vous au combat" (Whether light or heavy, march forth into battle), Caliph's communiqué, May 14. It appeared on May 15, 2015, on the Turkish jihadist site www.takvahaber.net.

9. Also, this caliphal appeal to enrollment: "Let Our Blood Be Our Wealth," in the governorship of Aleppo, April 27, 2015, archives of Combating Terrorism Center at West Point, available at www.ctc.usma.edu.

10. Jesse Singal, "Why ISIS Is So Terrifyingly Effective at Seducing New Recruits," *Science of Us*, August 18, 2014, available at www.nymag.com.

SIX
The Jihadist Aesthetic

1. Singal, "Why ISIS Is So Terrifyingly Effective."

2. On Al-Qaeda, see Nicholas J. O'Shaugnessy and Paul R. Baines, "Selling Terror: The Symbolisation and Positioning of Jihad." *Marketing Theory* 9, no. 2 (2009): 227–41.

3. *Dābiq* (in English; available at www.clarionproject.org); *Dābiq* and *ISN News* (in German; relatively easy Internet access); *Dār al-Islām* (in French; intermittent Internet access). Replaced, in five languages, by *Rumiyah* since September 2016 (Internet Archive, www.archive.org).

4. The Clarion Project, already mentioned, available at www.clarionproject.org.

5. French homeland security measures in force before the November 13, 2015, attack, known as Vigipirate (Prime Minister/SGDSN, January 17, 2014, non-classified information, available at www.sgdsn.gouv.fr), were reinforced by a new law on intelligence of May 2015 that gave the state additional surveillance and censorship powers; see www.stop-djihadisme.gouv.fr. From the night of the November 13, 2015, attack, a state of emergency, which has been renewed multiple times, has been in place, declared by the president and approved by the National Assembly. It has resulted in the deployment

of the Army on national soil, or OPINT ("operation interior" as opposed to OPEX, "operation exterior" or foreign deployment). OPINT is an unprecedented move in peacetime, which has transformed France into a theater of operations and brought the country close to the first step toward a declaration of war, being a state of *mise en garde* (preparedness to war, ahead of a general mobilization—or "on alert"), per the *Code de la défense*, article L2141-1.

6. Maha Hamdan, "Voices of Reason Fight to Be Heard in IS online propaganda war," February 22, 2015, www.linkedin.com.

7. Videos of atrocities are available at www.liveleak.com and www.bestgore.com; one can be viewed at Philippe-Joseph Salazar, "Défense de regarder: on égorge" (Don't look, we are slitting throats), *Les Influences*, August 29, 2014, available at www.lesinfluences.fr/Defense-de-regarder-on-egorge.html.

8. The khilafalive.info operation has apparently been up and running since January 2015. Adam Withnall, "Isis to Launch First 24-Hour Online TV Channel Featuring British Hostage John Cantlie and Flagship Show 'Time to Recruit,'" *The Independent*, May 11, 2015, available at www.independent.co.uk. Furthermore, a satellite television channel, Tawheed, is operating out of Libya.

9. "Islamic State Launches English-Language Radio Bulletins," Associated Press, April 7, 2015, available at www.publicopiniononline.com. Radio fm Al-Bayan, broadcasting from Mosul and local stations.

10. Angi English, "The Social Influence of ISIS Beheadings," *Homeland Security*, September 24, 2014, available at www.medium.com.

11. "Behind the Scenes—ISIS Beheadings Video," available at www.liveleak.com.

12. Specifically, www.bestgore.com combines extreme sex and violence.

13. Dounia Bouzar, Christophe Caupene, and Sulayman Valsan, *La Métamorphose opérée chez le jeune par les nouveaux discours terroristes* (The Operative Metamorphosis in a Young Person as a Result of the New Terrorist Discourse), Le Centre de Prévention contre les Dérives Sectaires liées à l'islam (CPDSI), 2014. Such programs, having first been hailed as a panacea, were subsequently beset with accusations of misappropriation of funds and either downgraded or closed down as state-sponsored projects in 2016. The Bouzar group focused on some eight hundred teenagers or young adults who had given signs of possible radicalization. A separate state project of 2016, aimed at establishing centers for the "reintegration into citizenry" of possible converts to jihadism and focusing on handfuls of individuals, has drawn much public criticism, following the launch of the first center in a Loire château, as wasteful posturing. "Un premier centre de déradicalisation ouvrira 'avant l'été,'" *Le Monde*, available at www.lemonde.fr/societe/article/2016/03/10/un-premier-centre-de-deradicalisation-ouvrira-avant-l-ete_4880551_3224.html.

14. Amaringsham, "Elton 'Ibrahim' Simpson's Path."

15. Frenchman Mohammed Mehra went on a killing rampage in the South of

France in 2012, having converted in 2008 and sworn allegiance to a pre-Caliphate organization known as Jund al-Kilafah.

16. On France and Belgium, see Collectif, *Les musulmans francophones, la compréhension, la terminologie, le discours* (Lyon: Tawhid, 2001), 97–103; on the United States, see the informative guides published by the Council on American-Islamic Relations, available at www.cair.com.

17. ISESCO, *Strategy of Islamic Cultural Action in the West*.

18. Aya Batrawy, Paisley Dodds, and Lori Hinnant, "'Islam For Dummies': IS Recruits Have Poor Grasp of Faith," Associated Press, August 15, 2015.

19. Aymenn Jawad Al-Tamimi, "We Have the Swords," May 2, 2015, available at www.aymennjawad.org/2015/05/we-have-the-swords-nasheed-from-islamic-state.

20. Makri, *Le Tajwîd*.

21. A counterpoint to the book by French moral philosopher Marcel Gauchet, *Le Désenchantement du monde. Une histoire politique de la religion* (The disenchantment of the world: A political history of religion) (Paris: Gallimard, 1985).

SEVEN

Caliphal Feminism

1. Debra Zedalis, *Female Suicide Bombers*, Strategic Studies Institute, U.S. Army War College, 2004, available at www.strategicstudiesinstitute.army.mil.

2. Hanna James, "Female Recruits to ISIS: The Recruiter's Veil," *Global News*, March 2015, available at www.globalnews.ca.

3. Géraldine Mossière, *Des femmes converties à l'islam en France et au Québec: religiosités d'un nouveau genre* (Women converted to Islam in France and in Quebec: A new genre of religiosity), doctoral thesis, University of Montreal, 2009.

4. Blandine Le Cain, "*Ligne 'anti-djihad': près de la moitié des appels concernent des femmes,*" (Anti-jihad phone line: More than half the calls are about women), *Le Figaro*, July 9, 2014, available at www.lefigaro.fr.

5. Soeren Kern, "Britain's Female Jihadists," *Gatestone Institute*, September 21, 2014, available at www.gatestoneinstitute.org.

6. Martin Evans, "Rotherham Sex Abuse Scandal: 1,400 Children Exploited by Asian Gangs While Authorities Turn a Blind Eye," *The Telegraph*, August 26, 2014, available at www.telegraph.co.uk.

7. Ellie Hall, "Gone Girl: An Interview with an American in ISIS," *BuzzFeed News*, April 18, 2015, available at www.buzzfeed.com; Martin Swant, "Family Spokesman: Alabama Woman Leaves to Join ISIS in Syria," *Yahoo News*, April 20, 2015, available at www.news.yahoo.com; Liam Stack, "Tashfeen Malik, Suspect in California Attack, Remains Mystery to Relatives," *New York Times*, December 5, 2015.

8. Julia Hoppemann, "Christin Converted to Islam," *Stern*, April 10, 2015, available at www.stern.de.

9. Marie-Estelle Pech, "En France, plus de femmes que d'hommes partent faire le djihad" (More women than men leave to undertake jihad in France), *Le Figaro*, April 15, 2015, available at www.lefigaro.fr. In March 2015: 136 women and 125 men.

10. Houria Alami M'Chichi, *Genre et politique au Maroc* (Gender and politics in Morocco) (Paris: L'Harmattan, 2002).

11. Stéphanie Latte Abdallah, "Les féminismes islamiques au tournant du xxiᵉ siècle" (Islamic feminisms at the turn of the 21st century), *Revue des mondes musulmans et de la Méditerranée* 28 (2010), available at http://remmm.revues.org/6822.

12. Charlie Winter, "Women of the Islamic State: A Manifesto on Woman by the Al-Khanssaa Brigade," *Quilliam*, 2015, available at www.quilliamfoundation.org.

13. *Dābiq*, no. 8, 2015, www.clarionproject.org.

14. Bilal Philips, *Salvation through Repentance* (Lyon: Tawhid, 1999), available at www.bilalphilips.com/wpcontent/uploads/2013/07/Salvation%20Through %20Repentance.pdf.

15. Jean Chélini et Henry Branthomme, *Histoire des pèlerinages non chrétiens* (History of non-Christian pilgrimages) (Paris: Hachette, 1987).

16. *Dār al-Islām*, January 2, 2015, 11.

17. ISESCO, *Strategy of Islamic Cultural Action in the West*.

18. ISESCO, *Strategy of Islamic Cultural Action in the West*, 57.

19. Brenda Stoter, "Radicalized Western Women Lead Children into Islamic State," *Al-Monitor*, April 13, 2015, available at www.al-monitor.com.

20. Joanna Paraszczuk, "More Than 330 Kyrgyz Said to Be Fighting Alongside IS in Syria, Iraq," Radio Free Europe, April 21, 2015, available at www.rferl.org. Zahava Moerdler, "Women and ISIS: Debunking the Myth of Gender and Violence," *Rights Wire*, March 24, 2015, available at www.rightswireblog.org.

21. Ahlam al-Nasr, poem cited in the *al-Quds al-Arabi* newspaper, October 14, 2014, revisited with detailed biographical analysis, "Ahlam al-Nasr: Islamic State's Jihadist Poetess," *Militant Leadership Monitor* 6, no. 6 (June 2015), available at www.jamestown.org.

EIGHT

Warrior Virility

1. In February 2016 there were more than four thousand American advisors on the ground. The number has increased since, due to the intensification of the war (Richard Sisk, "Number of US Troops in Iraq More Than 4,000," Military.com, February 3, 2016, available at www.military.com).

2. Video available at www.bestgore.com.

3. See the video mentioned in last note; see also Reid Standish, "Kazakh Child

Soldier Executes 'Russian Spies' in Islamic State Video," *Foreign Policy*, January 13, 2015, available at www.foreignpolicy.com.

4. *France Culture*, "Un Français converti à l'islam, Maxime Hauchard, bourreau djihadiste" (A Frenchman converted to Islam, Maxime Hauchard, jihadist henchman), *10 p.m. News*, November 17, 2014, available at www.franceculture.fr; *AFP*, "Le second bourreau djihadiste français 'en voie' d'être identifié" (The second French jihadist henchman "in the process of" being identified), *20 Minutes*, November 19, 2014, available at www.vingtminutes.fr.

5. See the debate between Farhad Khosrokhavar (author of *Radicalization: Why Some People Choose the Path of Violence*, New York, 2016) and the criminologist Jean-Pierre Bouchard (author of "Procès de Gilles Le Guen" (Trial of Gilles Le Guen), *Atlantico*, May 15, 2015, available at www.atlantico.fr).

6. Or OSINT. See Stevyn D. Gibson, "Open Source Intelligence: A Contemporary Intelligence Lifeline," doctoral thesis, Defense College of Management and Technology, Cranfield University, Cranfield, U.K., 2007.

7. Yannick Bressan, "DAESH ou le théâtre de la mort" (Daesh or the theater of death), Note de réflexion no. 18, Centre français de recherche sur le renseignement, 2015, available at www.cf2r.org; see also Christina Spens, "The Theatre of Cruelty: Dehumanization, Objectification, and Abu Ghraib," *Journal of Terrorism Research* 5, no. 3 (2014): 49–69.

8. For example Hamil Al-Bushra, *Les Loups solitaires ou les Lions de la ville* (Lone wolves or the lions of the city), 2015.

9. "Central Command Twitter Account Apparently Hacked by CyberCaliphate," RT, January 13, 2015, available at www.rt.com (Twitter hashtag #Cyber Caliphate).

10. For example, see American Department of State, *Designations of Foreign Terrorist Fighters*, September 24, 2014, available at www.state.gov.

11. Evan Bleier, "Behead Them in Their Own Homes: ISIS Publishes 'Kill List' Online of Names . . . ," *Daily Mail*, March 22, 2015, available at www.dailymail.co.uk.

12. Richard Nortob-Taylor, "Scale of UK Attacks on Islamic State in Iraq Revealed," *The Guardian*, May 11, 2015, available at www.theguardian.com.

13. Diane Maye, "We Know How to Strike, But Can We Achieve Victory? A Primer on the American Way of War in the 20th & 21st Centuries," *International Relations and Security Network Digital Library*, May 25, 2015, available at www.isn.ethz.ch.

14. Thomas E. Ricks, *Fiasco: The American Military Adventure in Iraq, 2003 to 2005* (New York: Penguin, 2007); Daren Bowyer, "Just War Doctrine: Relevance and Challenges in the 21st Century," doctoral thesis, Cranfield University, Cranfield, U.K., 2008.

15. James Der Derian, "Virtuous War/Virtual Theory," *International Affairs* 76, no. 4 (2000): 771–88, available at www.onlinelibrary.wiley.com.

16. Missy Ryan, "Gen. Dempsey's First Fight in Iraq Shapes His Approach to Islamic State," *Washington Post,* May 25, 2015, available at www.washington post.com; Julian Pecquet, "Congress Debates Greater U.S. Role in Iraq," *Al-Monitor,* May 21, 2015, available at www.al-monitor.com.

17. In Afghanistan, there were 10,548 civilian victims, of whom 3,699 were killed, in an annual increase of 25% in 2014. UN Aid Mission in Afghanistan, February 2015, available at www.un.org.

NINE

Islamic Porno-Politics

1. Yves Michaud, *Violence et politique* (Violence and Politics) (Paris: Gallimard, 1978). I am indebted to Michaud for his expression "porno-politics."

2. Hélène Lavoix, "The Islamic State Psyops," in three parts, *The Red (Team) Analysis Society,* February 9 and 23 and March 30, 2015, available at www.red analysis.org; Yannick Bressan, "La force des psyops de Daesh" (The strength of Daesh's psyops), Tribune libre no. 54, Centre français de recherche sur le renseignement, 2015, available at www.cf2r.org.

3. Henri Hubert and Marcel Mauss, *Essai sur la nature et la fonction du sacrifice* (Essay on the nature and the function of sacrifice), in Marcel Mauss, *Œuvres* (Paris: Minuit, 1968), I:193–307.

4. Daniel Sibony, *Le Groupe inconscient. Le lien et la peur* (The unconscious group: The bond and the power) (Paris: Christian Bourgois, 1980).

5. *Haunted Memories: The Islamic Republic's Executions of Kurds in 1979* (New Haven: Iran Human Rights Documentation Center, 2011), available at www.iran hrdc.org.

6. Pierre Legendre, *Jouir du pouvoir* (The pleasure of power) (Paris: Minuit, 1976).

7. Georges Dumézil, *Idées romaines* (Roman ideas) (Paris: Gallimard, 1969).

8. Vilfredo Pareto, *Traité de sociologie générale* (Treatise on general sociology) (Paris and Geneva: Vrin, 1968).

9. Philippe-Joseph Salazar, *L'Hyperpolitique, une passion française* (Hyperpolitics: A French passion) (Paris: Klincksieck, 2009).

10. James Foley's speech is published in *Dābiq,* August 3, 2014, 39, accompanied by a photograph of him looking thoughtful.

11. "Until There Came to Them Clear Evidence," video, April 19, 2015, available at https://shariaunveiled.wordpress.com/2015/04/19/islamic-state-new -release-until-there-came-to-them-clear-evidence-uncut-video.

12. Michel Foucault, *Discipline and Punish* (New York: Vintage, 1995).

13. Abderrahmane Moussaoui, "La politique de l'injure. Une décennie meurtrière en Algérie" (The politics of the insult: A murderous decade in Algeria), *Revue des mondes musulmans et de la Méditerranée* 103–104 (2004): 165–79.

14. Jean-Claude Milner, "La protection des populations et les limites du com-

passionnel" (The protection of populations and the limits of compassion), *Marianne*, February 10, 2015, available at www.marianne.net.

15. Sarah Dutton et al., "How Americans Are Feeling about the Fight against ISIS," CBS News, February 19, 2015, available at www.cbsnews.com.

TEN
Inexplicable Terrorist?

1. Jenell Johnson, "The Limits of Persuasion: Rhetoric and Resistance in the Last Battle of the Korean War," *Quarterly Journal of Speech* 100, no. 3 (2014): 323–47.

2. On Gilles Le Guen (the "atypical" individual that had joined al-Qaeda in the Maghreb), see "Gilles Le Guen, djihadiste français condamné à huit ans de prison" (Gilles Le Guen, French jihadist condemned to eight years in jail), *Atlantico*, May 15, 2015, available at www.atlantico.fr.

3. In the 1950s same rhetoric framed brainwashing and lobotomies. Jenell Johnson, *American Lobotomy: A Rhetorical History* (Ann Arbor: University of Michigan Press, 2014).

4. Thomson Reuters cable, December 7, 2013, APALERTTERROR 22:04:44 WLI-LAWSSCHOOLS.

5. On brainwashing as a talking point, see Sam Webb, "Jihadi Jake dead . . ." *The Mirror*, March 12, 2015, available at www.themirror.co.uk. For the low-end medical explanation, that Jihadi John had "bumped his head," see Anthony Bond, "Mohammed Emwazi: Jihadi John 'not the same again' after bumping his head during primary school fight," *The Mirror*, February 27, 2015, available at www.themirror.co.uk.

6. Michel Foucault, *Madness and Civilization: A History of Insanity in the Age of Reason* (New York: Vintage, 1988), and *Discipline and Punish*.

7. Paul Crozer, Asma Kaaniche, and Jan Lienard, "Nouvelle gouvernance à l'hôpital: recomposition de l'organisation et gestion des ressources humaines" (New governance at the hospital, recomposition of organization and human resources management), *Politiques et management public* 26, no. 2 (2008): 31–52, available at www.pmp.revues.org.

8. Arun Kundnani, "Radicalization: The Journey of a Concept," *Race and Class* 54, no. 2 (2012): 3–25.

9. Crowcroft, "Why Are So Many Young British Muslims."

10. Carole Piquet, "La France va créer un centre pour accompagner les jeunes de retour de Syrie ou d'Irak" (France is going to create a center to accompany youth returning from Syria or Iraq), *Le Figaro*, April 29, 2015, available at www.lefigaro.fr; Nick Logan, "Should Canada Try a Danish Plan to Deal with Radicals Returning from Syria?" *Global News*, October 21, 2014, available at www.globalnews.ca; Eugénie Bastié et al., "Un an après son lancement, bilan positif pour le numéro vert anti-jihad" (A year after its launch, positive

results for free emergency anti-jihad call-in number), *Le Figaro*, April 29, 2015, available at www.lefigaro.fr.

11. Clark McCauley and Sophia Moskalenko, "Mechanisms of Political Radicalization: Pathways toward Terrorism," *Terrorism and Political Violence* 20, no. 3 (2008): 415–33.

12. Anonymous, "Glossaire.DDE: le déterminisme-narrativiste" (DDE glossary: Narrativist determinism), *Dedefensa.org*, February 26, 2015, available at www .dedefensa.org; Thomas E. Ricks, "Some Thoughts on How to Change the Narrative on Violent Islamic Extremism," *Foreign Policy*, January 29, 2015, available at www.foreignpolicy.com. *The Virtual Caliphate* by Charlie Winter falls for the all-narrative (London: Quilliam Foundation, July 2015), available at www.quilliamfoundation.org.

13. Mercedes Garcia-Arenal, ed., *Conversions islamiques. Identités religieuses en islam méditerranéen* (Islamic conversions: Religious identities in Mediterranean Islam) Paris: Maisonneuve et Larose, 2001; *France Culture*, "Un Français converti à l'islam."

14. Amanda Giles, *Spiritual Intelligence*, Defence Academy of the United Kingdom, 2012, available at www.da.mod.uk.

15. Philips, *Salvation through Repentance*.

16. "Studies in Islamophobia" are being developed in American universities. Cinnamon Stillwell and Rima Greene, "Legitimizing Censorship: 'Islamophobia Studies' at Berkeley," *Jihad Watch*, May 23, 2015, available at www .jihadwatch.org.

17. Philippe-Joseph Salazar, "L'héroïsme de Djokhar Tsarnaev?" (The heroism of Djokhar Tsarnaev?), *Les Influences*, April 22, 2013, available at www.lesinflu ences.fr; James Dowling, Angus Thompson, and Tom Ninear, "Jake Bilardi Wrote about Terror and Death in his Online Blog"; Amaringsham, "Elton 'Ibrahim' Simpson's Path."

18. *The Just Balance*, Al Qistas ul Mustaqim, 1987, SH.

19. "Hors terrorisme, le témoignage de Mohamed Louizi" (Outside terrorism: The testimony of Mohamed Louizi) *Collège-Lycée Averroès de l'UOIF: l'arbre qui cache la forêt*, 2015, available at http://injonction.metaprojet.net. This lycée is a private Muslim secondary school (in France, as a rule private schools, which are not many in number and usually faith-based, remain under state supervision in order to protect republican secularism and to enforce a core curriculum aligned on state education).

20. On these two logics of social management, see Ernesto Laclau, "Populism: What's in a Name?" 32–49, in *Populism and the Mirror of Democracy*, ed. Francisco Panizza (London: Verso, 2005).

21. Caroline Beyer, "Détecter les candidats au djihad, c'est bien, les désendoctriner reste délicat" (Detecting candidates for jihad is good, un-indoctrinating them remains delicate), *Le Figaro*, June 2, 2014, available at www.lefigaro.fr.

22. Hollande, cited in *Le Monde*, "Comment le gouvernement compte lutter contre le djihad" (How the government intends to fight against jihad), April 22, 2014, available at www.lemonde.fr; see also the debate on the Prevent policy in Great Britain. Core document: "Prevent Strategy," Her Majesty's Government, 2001, available at www.official-documents.gov.uk.

23. The notion can be traced back to the UNESCO report on the radicalization of youth by violence. "The Manama Findings," UNESCO, June 2008.

24. See chapter 3, note 2. *Iftar with the Mujhahidden*, video, Furat Media, available at www.archive.org.

ELEVEN

How Our Discourse on Terror Is Controlled

1. Jethro Mullen, "Beheading of American Journalist James Foley Recalls Past Horrors," CNN, August 20, 2014, available at www.edition.cnn.com.

2. Bill Nichols, "Video Shows Beheading of American Captive," *USA Today*, November 5, 2004, available at www.usatoday.com.

3. Numerous videos on www.liveleak.com.

4. Adam Taylor and Sarah Kaplan, "Why Did Victims in Islamic State Beheading Video Look So Calm?" *Washington Post*, March 11, 2015, available at www.washingtonpost.com.

5. Michel Foucault, "The Discourse on Language," *The Archaeology of Knowledge and the Discourse on Language* (New York: Pantheon, 1971).

6. Philippe-Joseph Salazar, *L'Art de parler. Anthologie de manuels d'éloquence* (The art of speaking: An anthology of manuals of eloquence) (Paris: Klincksieck, 2003).

7. Salazar, *L'Art de parler*, section 41.

8. Colleen Derkatch and Judy Z. Segal, "Realms of Rhetoric in Health and Medicine," *Philosophy and Medicine* 82, no. 2 (2005): 138–42.

9. Updated regularly at *Political Geography Now*, www.polgeonow.com.

10. *St. John of Damascus on Islam, Heresy of the Ishmaelites*, Brill Academic Publishers, 1972.

TWELVE

Jihadist Populism

1. Michel Onfray, "Réflexions sur le peuple" (Reflections on the People), *Cahiers de psychologie sociale* 26 (2015), available at http://lodel.irevues.inist.fr/cahierspsychologiepolitique.

2. Ernesto Laclau, *On Populist Reason* (New York: Verso, 2007).

3. *Dār al-Islām*, January 2, 2015, 4.

4. *Dār al-Islām,* January 2, 2015, 2.
5. Bilardi, "From Melbourne to Ramadi."
6. Averroës, *Decisive Treatise and Epistle Dedicatory.*
7. Elliot Friedland, "Does ISIS Operate in the U.S. and Europe? We Analyze Islamic State's Modus Operandi in the West," *The Clarion Project,* May 10, 2015, available at www.clarionproject.org; "IS Says It Was Behind U.S. Prophet Cartoon Attack," BBC, May 5, 2015, available at www.bbc.com.
8. *Dābiq,* no. 10, p. 3, July 14, 2015, available at www.azelin.files.wordpress.com; *Islam Devleti . . . Seresi 1,* available at www.archive.org; Air Products, *Annual Report 2014,* available at www.airproducts.com.
9. The report delivered to the French prime minister by Member of Parliament S. Pietrasanta conforms to the managerial, sociological, psychological, medicalizing rationale denounced earlier by refusing to admit that jihadism is an uprising of a "people," anathema to socio-democratic ideology. *La Déradicalisation, outil de lutte contre le terrorisme* (Deradicalization, a tool in the fight against terrorism), June 2015.

THIRTEEN
A Radical Hostility

1. Carl Schmitt, *Theory of the Partisan: Intermediate Commentary on the Concept of the Political* (Candor, NY: Telos Press Publishing, 2007), 95.
2. Roger Trinquier, *La Guerre moderne* (Modern war) (Fort Leavenworth, KS: U.S. Army Command, Combat Studies Institute, 1985); David Galula, *Counterinsurgency Warfare* (London: Praeger, 1994); NATO, *Allied Joint Doctrine for Counterinsurgency (COIN),* AJP-3.4.4, 2011.
3. Some subheadings are drawn from Schmitt, *Theory of the Partisan,* 14, 78, 20, 32.
4. Brian Dodwell, "The Paris Attack: A Campaign and Its Goals," *CTC Sentinel* 8, no. 1 (January 2015), available at www.ctc.usma.edu.
5. This was written some fifteen months before the Nice, France, bus attack on July 14, 2016. It was based on car attacks that took place at Christmas time 2014 in the cities of Dijon and Nantes, France, with heavy casualties (23). The French government strenuously denied they were terrorist attacks, but terrorism experts dissented, referring to them as examples of a "low intensity permanent warfare."
6. Anonymous, "ISIS Supporter Threatens Wave of Terror Attacks in Major Western Cities, Offers Operational Advice to 'Lone Wolves,'" *MEMRI's Jihad and Terrorism Monitor,* January 22, 2015, available at www.memrijttm.org.
7. Gabriel Wermann, "Lone Wolves in Cyberspace," *Journal of Terrorism Research* 3, no. 2 (2012): 75–90.
8. Patrice Fluckiger, "Terrorisme. Après l'attaque vendredi d'un jeune militaire . . ." (Terrorism: After the Friday attack on a young military man), *Le Jour-*

nal de Saône-et-Loire, May 30, 2013, available at www.lejsl.com. Bruno Huet, "Un soldat du 3ᵉ RPIM menacé de mort" (A soldier of the 3rd Regiment of Marine Parachutists threatened with death), *La Dépêche*, January 10, 2015, available at www.ladepeche.fr; Jamey Keaten, "Trois soldats français attaqués au couteau" (Three French soldiers attacked with knives), *MSN Actualités*, February 3, 2015, available at www.msn.com.

9.   Audrey Kurth Cronin, "ISIS Is Not a Terrorist Group: Why Counterterrorism Won't Stop the Latest Jihadist Threat," *Foreign Affairs*, March–April 2015, available at www.foreignaffairs.com.

10.   French Defense Code, article L4111-1, "Status as a member of the armed forces requires under all circumstances a spirit of sacrifice, which may include the supreme sacrifice, discipline, availability, loyalty and neutrality."

11.   Lorenzo Vidino, "Sharia4: From confrontational activism to militancy," *Perspectives on Terrorism* 9, no. 2 (2015): 2–16.

12.   Ghaffar Hussein and Erin Marie Saltman, *Jihad Trending: A Comprehensive Analysis of Online Extremism and How to Counter It* (London: Quilliam, 2014), available at www.quilliamfoundation.org.

13.   *How to Survive in the West* e-book.

14.   See the report by Europol, *Changes in Modus Operandi of Islamic State (IS) Revisited*, Europol Public Information, the Hague, the Netherlands, November 2016.

15.   Anonymous, "Inside ISIS's Covert Ops," *Intelligence online*, no. 747, November 18, 2015, 2, available at www.intelligenceonline.com/archives/2015/11/18/num=747. Laurent Lagneau, "Selon le renseignement militaire, les jihadistes de Daesh peuvent communiquer sur Internet sans être détectés" (According to military intelligence the Daesh jihadists are able to communicate on the Internet without being detected), *Zone militaire*, May 6, 2015, available at www.opex360.com.

16.   Boston attack, 2013, condemned to death in May 2015.

17.   Soeren Kern, "Islamic State Supporters in Europe Fan Out, Plan Attacks," *The Clarion Project*, May 25, 2015, available at www.clarionproject.org.

18.   That there is no common term in use to categorize the partisan reveals a blind spot.

19.   Carl von Clausewitz, *On War*, Princeton University Press; Reprint edition (June 1, 1989).

20.   Исток, June 1, 2015.

21.   *Konstantiniyye*, June 1, 2015.

22.   "The Islamic State is an enemy like no other," quoted in Hannah Allam, "In Reversal, U.S. Official Admits Iraq Troops Reeling from Islamic State Offensive," *McClatchy DC*, May 20, 2015, available at www.mcclatchydc.com.

23.   Alexandre Mello and Michael Knights, "The Cult of the Offensive: The Islamic State on Defense," *CTC Sentinel*, April 30, 2015, available at www.ctc.usma.edu.

24. On the "Petraeus Doctrine," see Luke McCorkel, "The Development and Application of the 'Petraeus Doctrine' during the 2007 Iraq Troop 'Surge,'" thesis, University College, London, 2012, available at http://openscholarship .wustl.edu/etd/800. See also Brian Downing, "The Surge in Afghanistan," *The Agonist*, June 1, 2009, available at www.agonist.org.

25. James Rosen, "Ramadi Joins Lengthening List of Pentagon Misstatements on Iraq," *McClatchy DC*, May 18, 2015, available at www.mcclatchydc.com.

26. For the judgment of a Green Beret, see Mitchell Prothero, "Video of Islamic State Capabilities Impresses Military Experts," *McClatchy DC*, April 20, 2015, available at www.mcclatchydc.com; see also Gilles Munier, "Daech sera la première puissance militaire non-étatique opérationnelle au Maghreb en 2016," (Daesh will be the first non-state military power operating in the Maghreb in 2016), *Strategika 51*, March 9, 2015, available at www.strategika 51.wordpress.com. Laurent Touchard, *Organisation et méthodes de combat de l'État islamique* (The Islamic State's organization and methods of combat), May 2015, available at http://conops-mil.blogspot.fr/2015/05/revue-de-details -organisation-tactique.html.

27. "Adversaire proto-étatique d'un genre nouveau" (A new kind of proto-state adversary), summary to the Senate by General Christophe Gomart, director of military Intelligence, April 6, 2015, available at www.senat.fr. None of the senators touches the subject, except for the president of the commission, Mr. J.-P. Raffarin, who writes in conclusion, "Perhaps we should devote a morning's work to Daesh, this organization that's ending up resembling a state!"

28. Christoph Reuter, "The Terror Strategist: Secret Files Reveal the Structure of Islamic State," *Spiegel Online International*, April 18, 2015, available at www.spiegel.de.

29. Graeme Wood, "What ISIS Really Wants," *The Atlantic*, March 2015, available at theatlantic.com.

30. Sonia Le Gouriellec, *La Menace stratégique des États faibles. Quand les faits relativisent la théorie* (The Strategic Threat of Weak States: When Facts Relativize Theory), *IRSEM*, Note de recherche stratégique no. 18, April 2015.

31. Abu Rumaysah al Britani, *A Brief Guide to the Islamic State*, May 2015. A mark of statehood is the Caliphate's capacity to administer: Aymenn Jawad Al-Tamini, *Archive of Islamic State Administrative Documents*, available at www.ay mennjawad.org and "Research on the Islamic State," *Middle East Forum*, March 16–31, 2015, available at www.meforum.org. See also Carla E. Humud et al., *Islamic State Financing and U.S. Policy Approaches*, Congressional Research Service, April 10, 2015, available at www.crs.gov and the presentation by the hospital services *Health Diwan* in *Dābiq*, May 9, 2015, 24–26.

32. Jessica Lewis McFate, *The ISIS Defense in Iraq and Syria: Countering an Adaptive enemy*, "Hybridized Warfare" chapter, pp. 17–18, Institute for the Study of War, Washington, D.C., May 2015, available at www.understandingwar.org.

33. Bowyer, *Just War Doctrine*, ch. 4, "Issues of *Jus in Bello*."

34. In France: Alain Barluet, "Défense: 'Le territoire national devient une priorité stratégique'" (Defence: The National Territory Becomes a Strategic Priority), *Le Figaro*, video on Figaro TV, April 30, 2015, available at www.lefigaro.fr.

35. Anonymous, "Armée de terre française: retour sur le territoire" (French land forces: Return to the territory), *TTU Monde Arabe. Lettre hebdomadaire d'informations stratégiques*, no. 863, May 12, 2015, 6.

36. Friedland, "Does ISIS Operate in the U.S. and Europe?"; "IS Says It Was Behind U.S. Prophet Cartoon Attack," BBC.

37. Regarding this complex point, see Abu A'la Mawdudi, *Human Rights in Islam* (Lahore: Islamic Publications, 1995).

38. Jean-François Lyotard, *Differend: Phrases in Dispute* (Minneapolis: University of Minnesota Press, 1989).

EPILOGUE

Paris, November 13, 2015: A Comprehensive Lesson in Strategy

1. Ebi Spahiu, "Militant Islamists, Organized Crime and the Balkan Diaspora in Europe," *Terrorism Monitor* 13, no. 23, December 2, 2015, available at www.jamestown.org.

2. *The Washington Post* immediately gave a translation based, it would appear, on the Arabic version, which differs from the French version. See Philippe-Joseph Salazar, "La manipulation rhétorique" (Rhetorical manipulation), *Le Point*, no. 2254, November 19, 2015, 134–35, available at www.lepoint.fr.

3. Kevin Poireault, "Qui est Fabien Clain, la 'voix' de Daesh?" (Who is Fabien Clain, the "voice" of Daesh?), *Les Inrocks*, November 18, 2015, available at www.lesinrocks.fr.

4. *Dābiq*, no. 12, November 20, 2015, 25–28, available at www.clarionproject.org.

5. Umar abd al-Hakim (al-Shaykh Abu Mus'ab al-Souri), *The Call for a Global Islamic Resistance*, Part 2, "The Call, Program and Method," *The Military Theory of the Global Islamic Resistance Call*.

6. Sociologically in France distinctions are drawn among "the observant," "the faithful," and "Moslems by origin": The first group has grown from 36% to 42% since 2001. Michel Gurfinkiel, "After Paris are French Security sources up to the task?" *Middle East Forum*, November 19, 2015, www.meforum.org.

7. Friday Sermon, November 13, by the imam of the Aicha mosque in Montpellier, France, Mr. Mohamed Khattabi, eloquently explaining that the laws and customs of the West "cut one by one the limbs of the sleeping giant of Islam." Arab video, English translation available at www.memritv.org.

8. Seen on www.jihadology.net (videos regularly updated).

9. Sources available at www.trackingterrorism.org.

10. *Dār al-Islām*, no. 7, November 30, 2015, pp. 12–17.
11. *Dār al-Islām*, no. 7, November 30, 2015, p. 18.
12. *Der Gipfel des Islams Jihad* (The pinnacle of Islam's jihad). "No respite" is the name given the download by the site, available on www.archive.org, accessed November 24, 2015.
13. *The Media War upon the Islamic State: The Media Techniques of Misleading the Masses*, Ansar al-Khilafah, December 2, 2015, available at www.archives.org.
14. *Dābiq*, no. 15 ("Break the Cross"), July 31, 2016, 30–34, available at www.clarionproject.org.
15. *Dābiq*, no. 15 ("Break the Cross").
16. The title of Patricia Crone's fundamental work, *God's Rule*.
17. See chapter 4.
18. In the midst of military setbacks the Caliphate's propaganda remained on target, extolling its "methodology" of radical hostility and lambasting the "path of the deviants," that is, of those who deviate from their religious duty (*Rumiyah*, 7, March 7, 2017, 6–9).

Index

233

Index

Index

United States: anti-terrorism in, 178; female jihadists from, 100; founding of, 24–25; rhetorical response of, to Caliphate, 82–84; terror as defined in, 28; treason in, 51; universal ambitions of revolution in, 38–39

USSR. *See* Soviet Union

U.S. Code, 28, 51, 215n21. *See also* treason

U.S. State Department, 113

veiling, 99, 102, 108

videos: access to, 87–91; anti-jihadist, 60–69; of executions, 87–91, 110–11, 117–30, 147–49, 152–53, 156; goal of, 93; about November 13, 2015, attack, 196; propaganda, 213n26

violence, naming of, 171–72

virility, 109–16

virtuous war, 114

voluntarism, 158–60

wali (governor), 20–21

Wall Street Journal (newspaper), 16, 22

war: asymmetric, 113–14; Caliphate's conception of, 112–16, 180–82; nature of, 116; partisan warfare, 179–80; personalization of, 112–16; political worldview of Islam and, 22–23;

as politics by other means, 83, 179–83; refusal to acknowledge, 46, 51–52, 54–55, 60; rules of, 180–84; virtuous, 114; Western concept of, 113–15

war games, 181

wars of conquest, 182, 184–85

Washington, George, 17, 178

Western culture: Caliphate's relations with, 26, 157, 205; ceding of control of language by, 46–50; concept of war in, 113–15; digital fervor of, 58–60; feminism in, 106, 108; ideals and values of, 84–85, 91–92; inability of, to understand the Caliphate, 9, 10, 13–14, 154–55, 191; logic of, 8; polytheism of, 19; rhetoric and oratory of, 8, 9, 13, 112, 203–5. *See also* discourse, inadequacy of Western

White Terror (Russian Revolution), 41

"Why We Hate You & Why We Fight You," 199–201

women: autonomy of, 105–7; Caliphate and, 102–8; as jihadists, 99–108; as social question in France, 101–2; as suicide bombers, 99, 102

words. *See* language

Yemen, 23